Aunt Jane's Nieces In Society

Lyman Frank Baum

AUNT JANE'S NIECES
IN SOCIETY

AUNT JANE'S NIECES
IN SOCIETY

AUNT JANE'S NIECES
IN SOCIETY

EDITH VAN DYNE

AUTHOR OF "AUNT JANE'S NIECES," "AUNT
JANE'S NIECES ABROAD," "AUNT JANE'S
NIECES AT MILLVILLE," AND "AUNT
JANE'S NIECES AT WORK."

CHICAGO
THE REILLY & BRITTON CO.
PUBLISHERS

COPYRIGHT, 1910
BY
THE REILLY & BRITTON CO.

LIST OF CHAPTERS

AUNT JANE'S NIECES IN SOCIETY

CHAPTER I

UNCLE JOHN'S DUTY

"You're not doing your duty by those girls, John Merrick!"

The gentleman at whom this assertion was flung in a rather angry tone did not answer his sister-in-law. He sat gazing reflectively at the pattern in the rug and seemed neither startled nor annoyed. Mrs. Merrick, a pink-cheeked middle-aged lady attired in an elaborate morning gown, knitted her brows severely as she regarded the chubby little man opposite; then, suddenly remembering that the wrinkles might leave their dreadful mark on her carefully rolled and massaged features, she banished them with a pass of her ringed hand and sighed dismally.

"It would not have mattered especially had the poor children been left in their original condition of friendless poverty," she said. "They were then like a million other girls, content to struggle for a respectable livelihood and a doubtful position in the lower stratas of social communion. But you interfered. You came into their lives abruptly, appearing from those horrid Western wilds with an amazing accumulation of money and a demand that your three nieces become your special *protégées*. And what is the result?"

The little man looked up with a charming smile of good humored raillery. His keen gray eyes sparkled as mischievously as a schoolboy's. Softly he rubbed the palms of his hands together, as if enjoying the situation.

"What is it, Martha, my dear? What is the result?" he asked.

"You've raised them from their lowly condition to a sphere in which they reign as queens, the envy of all who know them. You've lavished your millions upon them unsparingly; they are not only presumptive heiresses but already possessed of independent fortunes. Ah, you think you've been generous to these girls; don't you, John Merrick?"

"Go on, Martha; go on."

"You've taken them abroad—you took my own daughter, John Merrick, and left *me* at home!— you've lugged your three nieces to the mountains and carried them to the seashore. You even encouraged them to enlist in an unseemly campaign to elect that young imbecile, Kenneth Forbes, and—"

"Oh, Martha, Martha! Get to the point, if you can. I'm going, presently."

"Not until you've heard me out. You've given your nieces every advantage in your power save one, and the neglect of that one thing renders futile all else you have accomplished."

Now, indeed, her listener seemed perplexed. He passed a hand over his shiny bald head as if to stimulate thought and exorcise bewilderment.

"What is it, then? What have I neglected?" was his mild enquiry.

"To give those girls their proper standing in society."

He started; smiled; then looked grave.

"You're talking foolishly," he said. "Why, confound it, Martha, they're as good girls as ever lived! They're highly respected, and—"

"Sir, I refer to Fashionable Society." The capitals indicate the impressive manner in which Mrs. Merrick pronounced those words.

"I guess money makes folks fashionable; don't it, Martha?"

"No, indeed. How ignorant you are, John. Can you not understand that there is a cultured, aristocratic and exclusive Society in New York that millions will not enable one to gain *entrèe* to?"

"Oh, is there? Then I'm helpless."

"You are not, sir."

"Eh? I thought you said—"

"Listen, John; and for heaven's sake try for once to be receptive. I am speaking not only for the wellfare of my daughter Louise but for Beth and Patricia. Your nieces are charming girls, all three. With the advantages you have given them they may well become social celebrities."

"H-m-m. Would they be happier so?"

"Of course. Every true woman longs for social distinction, especially if it seems difficult to acquire. Nothing is dearer to a girl's heart than to win acceptance by the right social set. And New York society is the most exclusive in America."

"I'm afraid it will continue to exclude our girls, Martha."

"Not if you do your duty, John."

"That reminds me. What is your idea of my duty, Martha? You've been talking in riddles, so far," he protested, shifting uneasily in his chair.

"Let me explain more concisely, then. Your millions, John Merrick, have made you really famous, even in this wealthy metropolis. In the city and at your club you must meet with men who have the *entrée* to the most desirable social circles; men who might be induced to introduce your nieces to their families, whose endorsement would effect their proper presentation."

"Nonsense."

"It is n't nonsense at all."

"Then blamed if I know what you're driving at."

"You're very obtuse."

"I won't agree to that till I know what 'obtuse' means. See here, Martha; you say this social position, that the girls are so crazy for—but they've never said anything to *me* about it—can't be bought. In the next breath you urge me to buy it. Phoo! You're a thoughtless, silly woman, Martha, and let your wild ambitions run away with your common sense."

Mrs. Merrick sighed, but stubbornly maintained her position.

"I don't suggest 'buying' such people; not at all, John. It's what is called—ah—ah—'influence'; or, or—"

"Or 'pull.' 'Pull' is a better word, Martha. Do you imagine there's any value in social position that can be acquired by 'pull'?"

"Of course. It has to be acquired some way— if one is not born to it. As a matter of fact, Louise is entitled, through her connection with *my* family—"

"Pshaw, I knew *your* family, Martha," he interrupted. "An arrant lot of humbugs."

"John Merrick!"

"Don't get riled. It's the truth. I *knew* 'em. On her father's side Louise has just as much to brag about—an' no more. We Merricks never amounted to much, an' did n't hanker to trip the light fantastic in swell society. Once, though, when I was a boy, I had a cousin who spelled down the whole crowd at a spellin'-bee. We were quite proud of him then; but he went wrong after his triumph, poor fellow! and became a book agent. Now, Martha, I imagine this talk of yours is all hot air, and worked off on me not because the girls want society, but because you want it for 'em. It's all *your* ambition, I'll bet a peanut."

"You misjudge me, as usual, John. I am urging a matter of simple justice. Your nieces are lovely girls, fitted to shine in any sphere of life," she continued, knowing his weak point and diplomatically fostering it. "Our girls have youth, accomplishments, money—everything to fit them for social triumphs. The winter season is now approaching; the people are flocking back to town from their country homes; fashionable gaieties and notable events will soon hold full sway. The dear girls are surely entitled to enjoy these things, don't you think? Aren't they worthy the best that life has to offer? And why shouldn't they enter society, if you do your full duty? Once get them properly introduced and they will be able to hold their own with perfect ease. Give me the credit for knowing these things, John, and try to help your nieces to attain their ambition."

"But *is* it their ambition?" he asked, doubtfully.

"They have not said so in words; but I can assure you it *is* their ambition, because all three are sensible, spirited, young women, who live in this age and not the one you yourself knew a half century or so ago."

Mr. Merrick sighed and rubbed his head again. Then he slowly rose.

"Mornin', Martha," he said, with a somewhat abstracted nod at his sister-in-law. "This is a new idea to me. I'll think it over."

CHAPTER II

A QUESTION OF "PULL"

John Merrick's face was not so cheery as usual as he made his way into the city. This suggestion of Martha Merrick's regarding his inattention to duty to his beloved nieces was no easy nut to crack.

He knew his sister-in-law to be a wordly-minded, frivolous woman, with many trivial ambitions; but in this instance he had misgivings that she might be right. What did he, John Merrick, know of select society? A poor man, of humble origin, he had wandered into the infantile, embryo West years ago and there amassed a fortune. When he retired and returned to "civilization" he found his greatest reward in the discovery of three charming nieces, all "as poor as Job's turkey" but struggling along bravely, each in her individual characteristic way, and well worthy their doting uncle's affectionate admiration. Mrs. Merrick had recited some of the advantages they had derived from the advent of this rich relative; but even she could not guess how devoted the man was to the welfare of these three fortunate girls, nor how his kindly, simple heart resented the insinuation that he was neglecting anything that might contribute to their happiness.

Possession of money had never altered John Merrick's native simplicity. He had no extravagant tastes, dressed quietly and lived the life of the people. On this eventful morning the man of millions took a cross-town car to the elevated station and climbed the stairs to his train. Once seated and headed cityward he took out his memorandum book to see what engagements he had for the day. There were three for the afternoon. At twelve o'clock he had promised to meet Von Taer.

"H-m-m. Von Taer."

Gazing reflectively from the window he remembered a conversation with a prominent banker some month or so before. "Von Taer," the banker had said, "is an aristocrat with an independent fortune, who clings to the brokerage business because he inherited it from his father and grandfather. I hold that such a man has no moral right to continue in business. He should retire and give the other fellow a chance."

"Why do you call him an aristocrat?" Mr. Merrick had enquired.

"Because his family is so ancient that it shames the ark itself. I imagine his ancestors might have furnished Noah the lumber to build his ship. In New York the '400' all kowtow to Von Taer."

"Seems to me he has the right to be a broker if he wants to," asserted Mr. Merrick.

"The right; yes. But, between us, Mr. Merrick, this society swell has no mental capacity to handle such an uncertain business. He's noted for doing unwarranted things. To me it's a marvel that Von Taer hasn't shipwrecked the family fortunes long ago. Luck has saved him, not foresight."

That speech of a few weeks ago now seemed prophetic to John Merrick. Within a few days the aristocratic broker had encountered financial difficulties and been forced to appeal to Mr. Merrick, to whom he obtained an introduction through a mutual friend. Von Taer was doubtless solvent, for he controlled large means; but unless a saving hand was extended at this juncture his losses were sure to be severe, and might even cripple him seriously.

All this Mr. Merrick shrewdly considered in the space of a few moments. As he left the train he looked at his watch and found it was barely eleven. He decided not to await the hour of appointment. With his usual brisk stride he walked to Von Taer's offices and was promptly admitted to the broker's sanctum.

Hedrik Von Taer was a fine looking man, tall, grave, of dignified demeanor and courteous manners. He stood until his visitor was seated and with a gesture of deference invited him to open the conversation.

"I've decided to make you the loan, Von Taer," began Mr. Merrick, in his practical, matter-of-fact way. "Three hundred thousand, wasn't it?

Call on Major Doyle at my office this afternoon and he'll arrange it for you."

An expression of relief crossed the broker's face.

"You are very kind, sir," he answered. "I assure you I fully appreciate the accommodation."

"Glad to help you," responded the millionaire, briskly. Then he paused with marked abruptness. It occurred to him he had a difficult proposition to make to this man. To avoid the cold, enquiring eyes now fixed upon him he pulled out a cigar and deliberately cut the end. Von Taer furnished him a match. He smoked a while in silence.

"This loan, sir," he finally began, "is freely made. There are no strings tied to it. I don't want you to feel I'm demanding any sort of return. But the truth is, you have it in your power to grant me a favor."

Von Taer bowed.

"Mr. Merrick has generously placed me under an obligation it will afford me pleasure to repay," said he. But his eyes held an uneasy look, nevertheless.

"It's this way," explained the other: "I've three

nieces—fine girls, Von Taer—who will some day inherit my money. They are already independent, financially, and they're educated, well-bred and amiable young women. Take my word for it."

"I am sure your statements are justified, Mr. Merrick." Yet Hedrik Von Taer's face, usually unexpressive, denoted blank mystification. What connection could these girls have with the favor to be demanded?

"Got any girls yourself, Von Taer?"

"A daughter, sir. My only child.

"Grown up?"

"A young lady now, sir."

"Then you'll understand. I'm a plain uneducated man myself. Never been any nearer swell society than a Fifth Avenue stage. My money has given me commercial position, but no social one worth mentioning. Your '400's' a bunch I can't break into, nohow."

A slight smile hovered over the other's lips, but he quickly controlled it.

"They tell me, though," continued the speaker, "that *your* family has long ago climbed into the top notch of society. You're one o' the big guns in the battery, an' hold the fort against all comers."

Von Taer merely bowed. It was scarcely necessary to either admit or contradict the statement. Uncle John was a little indignant that his companion showed no disposition to assist him in his explanation, which a clear head might now easily comprehend. So, with his usual frankness, he went directly to the point.

"I'd like my girls to get into the best—the most select—circles," he announced. "They're good and pretty and well-mannered, so it strikes me they're entitled to the best there is a-going. I don't want to mix with your swell crowd myself, because I ain't fit; likewise the outfit ain't much to my taste, askin' your pardon; but with women it's different. They need to stand high an' shine bright to make 'em really happy, and if any special lot is particularly ex-clusive an' high-falutin', that's the crowd they long to swarm with. It's human nature—female human nature, anyhow. You catch my idea, Von Taer, don't you?"

"I think so, Mr. Merrick. Yet I fail to see

how I can be of service to you in gratifying the ambition of your charming nieces."

"Then I'll go, and you may forget what I've said." The visitor arose and took his hat from the table. "It was only a fool notion, anyway; just a thought, badly expressed, to help my girls to a toy that money can't buy."

Hedrik Von Taer gazed steadily into the man's face. There was something in the simple, honest self-abnegation of this wealthy and important person that won the respect of all he met. The broker's stern eyes softened a bit as he gazed and he allowed a fugitive smile, due to his own change of attitude, to wreathe his thin lips again—just for an instant.

"Sit down, please, Mr. Merrick," he requested, and rather reluctantly Uncle John resumed his seat. "You may not have an especially clear idea of New York society, and I want to explain my recent remark so that you will understand it. What is called 'the 400' may or may not exist; but certainly it is no distinct league or association. It may perhaps be regarded as a figure of speech, to indicate how few are really admitted to the most exclusive circles. Moreover, there can be no dominant 'leader of society' here, for the reason that not all grades of society would recognize the supremacy of any one set, or clique. These cliques exist for various reasons. They fraternize generally, but keep well within their own circles. Kindred tastes attract some; ancient lineage others. There is an ultra-fashionable set, a sporting set, a literary set, an aristocratic set, a rather 'fast' set, a theatrical set—and so on. These may all lay claim with certain justice to membership in good society. Their circles are to an extent exclusive, because some distinction must mark the eligibility of members. And outside each luminous sphere hovers a multitude eager to pass the charmed circle and so acquire recognition. Often it is hard to separate the initiate from the uninitiate, even by those most expert. Is it difficult to comprehend such a condition as I have described, Mr. Merrick?"

"Somewhat, Mr. Von Taer. The wonder to me is why people waste time in such foolishness."

"It is the legitimate occupation of many; the folly of unwise ambition impels others. There is a fascination about social life that appeals to the majority of natures. Let us compare society to a mountain whose sides are a steep incline, difficult to mount. To stand upon the summit, to become the cynosure of all eyes, is a desire inherent, seemingly, in all humanity; for humanity loves distinction. In the scramble toward the peak many fall by the wayside; others deceive themselves by imagining they have attained the apex when they are far from it. It is a game, Mr. Merrick, just as business is a game, politics a game, and war a game. You know how few really win."

"Here," said Uncle John, musingly, "is a philosophy I did not expect from you, Von Taer. They tell me you're one who stands on top the peak. And you were born that way, and didn't have to climb. Seems to me you rather scorn the crowd that's trying to climb to an eminence you never had to win. That wouldn't be my way. And I suspect that if the crowd wasn't trying to climb to you, your own position wouldn't be worth a cotton hat."

Von Taer had no answer to this criticism.

Perhaps he scarcely heard it, for he appeared lost in a brown study. Finally he said:

"Will you permit my daughter to call upon your nieces, Mr. Merrick?"

"Of course, sir."

"Then kindly give me their addresses."

Uncle John wrote them on a slip of paper.

"You may now dismiss the subject from your mind, sir, as you lately advised me to do. Whatever may be accomplished in the direction you have suggested I will gladly undertake. If I succeed it will be exceedingly gratifying to us all, I am sure."

Mr. Merrick left the office in a rather humbled and testy mood. He disliked to ask favors at any time and now felt that he had confided himself to the mercy of this callous aristocrat and met with a distinct rebuff.

But he had done it for the sake of his beloved nieces—and they would never know what humiliation this unsatisfactory interview had cost him.

CHAPTER III

DIANA

Diana Von Taer can not be called a type. She was individual. Aristocratic to her finger tips, she was unlike all other aristocrats. An admitted queen of society, her subjects were few and indifferent. She possessed ancient lineage, was highly accomplished, had been born to the purple, as the saying is; but none of these things conspired to make her the curious creature she was.

As we make her acquaintance she is twenty-three years of age—and looks eighteen. She is tall and slender and carries her handsome form with exquisite grace. Diana is never abrupt; her voice is ever modulated to soft, even tones; she rises from a chair or couch with the lithe, sinuous motion of a serpent uncoiling.

Her face, critically regarded, is not so admirable as her form. The features are a trifle too elongated, and their delicacy is marred by a nose a bit broad and unshapely and a mouth with thin lips primly set. Her dark eyes might be magnificent if wide open; but through the narrow slits of their lids, half hidden by long curling lashes, the eyes peer at you with a cold, watchful, intent gaze that carries a certain uncanny and disconcerting fascination.

Yet the girl is essentially feminine. If you refrain from meeting that discomfiting gaze—and her familiars have learned to avoid it—Diana impresses you as being graceful, dainty and possessed of charming manners. Her taste in dress is perfect. She converses fluently on many topics. It is her custom to rise at ten o'clock, whatever time she may have retired the night before; to read until luncheon; to devote the remainder of her day to the requirements of society.

Eligible young men of admitted social standing call upon Diana at such intervals as the proprieties require. They chatter "small talk" and are careful to address her with deference. With an exception to be referred to later these young men have no more thought of "flirting" with Miss Von

Taer than they would with the statue of the goddess, her namesake. Her dinner parties and entertainments are very successful. She is greatly admired, *per se,* but has no intimate friends.

When her mother died, some years before, an aunt had come to live with Diana, and now posed as her chaperone. Mrs. Cameron was a stolid, corpulent lady, with a countenance perpetually placid and an habitual aversion to displaying intellect. Her presence in the establishment, although necessary, was frankly ignored. Fortunately she never obtruded herself.

Hedrik Von Taer was passionately devoted to his daughter. He alone, perhaps, of all the world, thoroughly understood her and appreciated her talents. She may have frightened him at times, but that only added to his admiration. In return Diana displayed a calm, but affectionate regard for her father.

Often after dinner these two would pass an hour together in a corner of the drawing-room, where the cold gray eyes of the man met the intent, half-veiled glance of the girl with perfect understanding. They talked of many things, including business. Hedrik had no secrets from his daughter.

The desperate condition of his finances, when he had been caught in a "corner" on wheat and nearly crushed, had not dismayed her in the least. It was she who had counseled him to appeal to John Merrick, since the name and fame of the eccentric millionaire were familiar to her as to him.

He related to Diana his interview with Mr. Merrick on his return home. He was saved. The three hundred thousand were now in the bank to his credit and he could weather the coming storm easily—perhaps with profit. In a tone half amused, half serious, he told her of the little millionaire's desire to secure *entrée* into good society for his three nieces.

Diana laughed with her lips; her eyes never laughed. Then she took in her hand the paper containing the addresses of the three girls and regarded it thoughtfully.

"It is a curious request, *mon pere*," she said, in her soft, even tones; "but one we cannot diplomatically disregard. Provided, however—"

"Yes, Diana;" as she paused.

"Provided these prospective *debutantes* are not wholly impossible."

"I realize that," returned her father. "John Merrick is a great power in the city. He has been useful to me, and may be again. I have this chance to win him. But the man is very common clay, despite his wealth, and his three nieces are likely to be made of the same material. Should they prove impossible you cannot well descend to introducing them to our set."

"I am not certain of that, sir," said the girl, with a pretty shrug. "My position is too secure to be jeopardized by any error of this sort. I believe I may introduce these girls without risk. I shall not vouch for them too strongly, and after their debut they must stand or fall on their own merits."

"It is something a Von Taer has never yet done," remarked the man, gravely.

"To commercialize his social position? But, father dear, the age is fast commercializing everything. I think our especial set is as yet comparatively free from contamination by the 'lately rich'; but even among us money has glossed many offenses that a generation ago would have meant social ostracism."

He nodded.

"That is true, Diana."

"Life with me is a bit dull, as well. Everlasting routine, however admirable, is tiresome. I scent amusement in this adventure, which I have decided to undertake. With your permission I will see these girls and quickly decide their fate. Should they prove not too dreadfully *outré* you may look to see them my especial *protégés*."

"I leave all to your discretion, Diana," returned Von Taer, with a sigh. "If, in the end, some of the more particular venture to reproach you—"

"It will not matter," interrupted the daughter, lightly, as her dark eyes narrowed to a hair's breadth. "Any who dares reproach Diana Von Taer will afford her interesting occupation. And to offset that remote contingency we shall permanently enslave the powerful John Merrick. I understand he is hard as nails in financial matters; but to us the man has disclosed his one weakness

33

—ambition to promote his three nieces. Since we have discovered this vulnerable point, let us take advantage of it. I am satisfied the loan of three hundred thousand was but a lure—and how cleverly the man gauged us!"

Von Taer scowled.

"Get your wraps, Diana. The carriage is waiting, and we are due at Mrs. Doldringham's crush."

CHAPTER IV

THE THREE NIECES

The Von Taers did not affect motor cars. In some circles the carriage and pair is still considered the more aristocratic mode of conveyance. Established customs do not readily give way to fads and freaks.

Consulting her memoranda as she rode along in her handsome, tastefully appointed equipage, Diana found that Louise Merrick, one of the three girls she had set out to discover, was the nearest on her route. Presently she rang the bell at the Merrick residence, an eminently respectable dwelling in a desirable neighborhood.

Diana could not resist a sigh of relief as her observant glance noted this detail. A dignified butler ushered her into a reception room and departed with her card.

It was now that the visitor's nose took an up-

ward tendency as she critically examined her surroundings. The furnishings were abominable, a
mixture of distressingly new articles with those
evidently procured from dealers in "antiquities."
Money had been lavished here, but good taste
was absent. To understand this—for Miss Von
Taer gauged the condition truly—it is necessary
to know something of Mrs. Martha Merrick.

This lady, the relict of John Merrick's only
brother, was endowed with a mediocre mind and
a towering ambition. When left a widow with
an only daughter she had schemed and contrived
in endless ways to maintain an appearance of com-
petency on a meager income. Finally she divided
her capital, derived from her husband's life insur-
ance, into three equal parts, which she determined
to squander in three years in an attempt to hood-
wink the world with the belief that she was
wealthy. Before the three years were ended her
daughter Louise would be twenty, and by that
time she must have secured a rich *parti* and been
safely married. In return for this "sacrifice" the
girl was to see that her mother was made comfortable thereafter.

This worldly and foolish design was confided to Louise when she was only seventeen, and her unformed mind easily absorbed her mother's silly ambition. It was a pity, for Louise Merrick possessed a nature sweet and lovable, as well as instinctively refined—a nature derived from her dead father and with little true sympathy with Mrs. Merrick's unscrupulous schemes. But at that age a girl is easily influenced, so it is little wonder that under such tuition Louise became calculating, sly and deceitful, to a most deplorable degree.

Such acquired traits bade fair in the end to defeat Mrs. Merrick's carefully planned *coup,* for the daughter had a premature love affair with a youth outside the pale of eligibility. Louise ignored the fact that he had been disinherited by his father, and in her reckless infatuation would have sacrificed her mother without thought of remorse. The dreadful finale had only been averted by the advent of Uncle John Merrick, who had changed the life plans of the widow and her heedless daughter and promptly saved the situation.

John Merrick did not like his sister-in-law, but he was charmed by his lovely niece and took her at once to his affectionate old heart. He saw the faults of Louise clearly, but also appreciated her sweeter qualities. Under his skillful guidance she soon redeemed herself and regained control of her better nature. The girl was not yet perfect, by any means; she was to an extent artificial and secretive, and her thoughtless flirtations were far from wise; but her two cousins and her uncle had come to know and understand her good points. They not only bore patiently with her volatile nature but strove to influence her to demonstrate her inherent good qualities.

In one way her mother's calculating training had been most effective. Louise was not only a dainty, lovely maid to the eye, but her manners were gracious and winning and she had that admirable self-possession which quickly endears one even to casual acquaintances. She did not impress more intimate friends as being wholly sincere, yet there was nothing in her acts, since that one escapade referred to, that merited severe disapproval.

Of course the brilliant idea of foisting her precious daughter upon the "select" society of the metropolis was original with Mrs. Merrick. Louise was well content with things as they were; but not so the mother. The rise from poverty to affluence, the removal of all cares and burdens from her mind, had merely fostered still greater ambitions. Uncle John's generosity had endowed each of his three nieces with an ample fortune. "I want 'em to enjoy the good things of life while they're at an age to enjoy 'em," he said; "for the older one gets the fewer things are found to be enjoyable. That's my experience, anyhow." He also told the girls frankly that they were to inherit jointly—although not equally—his entire fortune. Yet even this glowing prospect did not satisfy Mrs. Merrick. Since all her plans for Louise, from the very beginning, had been founded on personal selfishness, she now proposed to have her daughter gain admission to recognized fashionable society in order that she might herself bask in the reflection of the glory so obtained and take her place with

the proud matrons who formed the keystone of
such society.

After carefully considering ways and means
to gain her object she had finally conceived the
idea of utilizing Mr. Merrick. She well knew
Uncle John would not consider one niece to the
exclusion of the others, and had therefore used
his influence to get all three girls properly "introduced." Therefore her delight and excitement were intense when the butler brought up
Diana's card and she realized that "the perfectly
swell Miss Von Taer" was seated in her reception room. She rushed to Louise, who, wholly
innocent of any knowledge of the intrigue which
had led to this climax, opened her blue eyes in
astonishment and said with a gasp:

"Oh, mother! what shall I do?"

"Do? Why, go down and make yourself
agreeable, of course. It's your chance, my dear,
your great chance in life! Go—go! Don't, for
heaven's sake, keep her waiting."

Louise went down. In her most affable and
gracious way she approached the visitor and said:

"It is very nice of you to call upon me. I am *so* glad to meet Miss Von Taer."

Diana, passing conversational nothings with the young girl, was pleased by her appearance and self-possession. This aspirant for social honors was fresh, fair and attractive, with a flow of small talk at her tongue's end.

"Really," thought the fastidious visitor, "this one, at least, will do me no discredit. If she is a fair sample of the others we shall get along very nicely in this enterprise."

To Louise she said, before going:

"I'm to have an evening, the nineteenth. Will you assist me to receive? Now that we are acquainted I wish to see more of you, my dear, and I predict we shall get along famously together."

The girl's head swam. Help Miss Von Taer to receive! Such an honor had been undreamed of an hour ago. But she held her natural agitation under good control and only a round red spot upon each cheek betrayed her inward excitement as she prettily accepted the invitation. Beneath their drooping lashes Diana's sagacious eyes read the thoughts of the girl quite accurately. Miss

Von Taer enjoyed disconcerting anyone in any way, and Louise was so simple and unsophisticated that she promised to afford considerable amusement in the future.

By the time Diana had finished her brief call this singular creature had taken the measure of Louise Merrick in every detail, including her assumption of lightness and her various frivolities. She understood that in the girl were capabilities for good or for evil, as she might be led by a stronger will. And, musingly, Diana wondered who would lead her.

As for Louise, she was enraptured by her distinguished visitor's condescension and patronage, and her heart bounded at the thought of being admitted to the envied social coterie in which Diana Von Taer shone a bright, particular star.

The second name in the list of John Merrick's nieces was that of Elizabeth De Graf. She lived at a good private hotel located in an exclusive residence district.

It was true that Elizabeth—or "Beth," as she was more familiarly called—was not a permanent guest at this hotel. When in New York she was

accustomed to live with one or the other of her
cousins, who welcomed her eagerly. But just
now her mother had journeyed from the old Ohio
home to visit Beth, and the girl had no intention
of inflicting her parent upon the other girls.
Therefore she had taken rooms at the hotel tem-
porarily, and the plan suited her mother excel-
lently. For one thing, Mrs. De Graf could go
home and tell her Cloverton gossips that she had
stopped at the most "fashionable" hotel in New
York; a second point was that she loved to feast
with epicurean avidity upon the products of a
clever *chef*, being one of those women who live
to eat, rather than eat to live.

Mrs. De Graf was John Merrick's only surviv-
ing sister, but she differed as widely from the
simple, kindly man in disposition as did her in-
genious daughter from her in mental attainments.
The father, Professor De Graf, was supposed to
be a "musical genius." Before Beth came into
her money, through Uncle John, the Professor
taught the piano and singing; now, however, the
daughter allowed her parents a liberal income,
and the self-engrossed musician devoted himself

to composing oratorios and concertas which no one but himself would ever play.

To be quite frank, the girl cared little for her gross and selfish parents, and they in turn cared little for her beyond the value she afforded them in the way of dollars and cents. So she had not lived at home, where constant quarrels and bickerings nearly drove her frantic, since Uncle John had adopted her. In catering to this present whim of her mother, who longed to spend a few luxurious weeks in New York, Beth sacrificed more than might be imagined by one unacquainted with her sad family history.

Whimsical Major Doyle often called Uncle John's nieces "the Three Graces"; but Beth was by odds the beauty of them all. Splendid brown eyes, added to an exquisite complexion, almost faultless features and a superb carriage, rendered this fair young girl distinguished in any throng. Fortunately she was as yet quite unspoiled, being saved from vanity by a morbid consciousness of her inborn failings and a sincere loathing for the moral weakness that prevented her from correcting those faults. Judging Beth by the common

44

standard of girls of her age, both failings and
faults were more imaginary than real; yet it was
her characteristic to suspect and despise in herself
such weaknesses as others would condone, or at
least regard leniently. For here was a girl true
and staunch, incapable of intrigue or deceit, frank
and outspoken, all these qualities having been
proven more than once. Everyone loved Beth
De Graf save herself, and at this stage of her
development the influence of her cousins and of
Uncle John had conspired to make the supersen-
sitive girl more tolerant of herself and less morbid
than formerly.

I think Beth knew of Diana Von Taer, for the
latter's portrait frequently graced the society
columns of the New York press and at times the
three nieces, in confidential mood, would canvass
Diana and her social exploits as they did the acts
of other famous semi-public personages. But the
girl had never dreamed of meeting such a celeb-
rity, and Miss Von Taer's card filled her with
curious wonder as to the errand that had brought
her.

The De Grafs lived *en suite* at the hotel, for

Beth had determined to surround her Sybaritic mother with all attainable luxury, since the child frequently reproached herself with feeling a distinct repulsion for the poor woman. So to-day Diana was ushered into a pretty parlor where Beth stood calmly awaiting her.

The two regarded one another in silence a moment, Miss De Graf's frank eyes covering the other with a comprehensive sweep while Miss Von Taer's narrowed gaze, profoundly observant, studied the beautiful girl before her with that impenetrable, half-hidden gleam that precluded any solution.

"Miss Von Taer, I believe," said Beth, quietly glancing at the card she held. "Will you be seated?"

Diana sank gracefully into a chair. The sinuous motion attracted Beth's attention and gave her a slight shiver.

"I am so glad to meet you, my dear," began the visitor, in soft, purring accents. "I have long promised myself the pleasure of a call, and in spite of many procrastinations at last have accomplished my ambition."

Beth resented the affectation of this prelude, and slightly frowned. Diana was watching; she always watched.

"Why should you wish to call upon me?" was the frank demand. "Do not think me rude, please; but I am scarcely in a position to become a desirable acquaintance of Miss Von Taer." The tone was a trifle bitter, and Diana noted it. A subtile antagonism seemed springing up between them and the more experienced girl scented in this danger to her plans. She must handle this young lady more cautiously than she had Louise Merrick.

"Your position is unimpeachable, my dear," was the sweet-toned response. "You are John Merrick's niece."

Beth was really angry now. She scowled, and it spoiled her beauty. Diana took warning and began to think quickly.

"I referred to my social position, Miss Von Taer. Our family is honest enough, thank God; but it has never been accepted in what is termed select society."

Diana laughed; a quiet, rippling laugh as icy

as a brook in November, but as near gaiety as she could at the moment accomplish. When she laughed this way her eyes nearly closed and became inscrutable. Beth had a feeling of repulsion for her caller, but strove to shake it off. Miss Von Taer was nothing to her; could be nothing to her.

"Your uncle is a very wealthy man," said Diana, with easy composure. "He has made you an heiress, placing you in a class much sought after in these mercenary days. But aside from that, my dear, your personal accomplishments have not escaped notice, and gossip declares you to be a very fascinating young woman, as well as beautiful and good. I do not imagine society claims to be of divine origin, but were it so no one is more qualified to grace it."

The blandishments of this speech had less effect upon Beth than the evident desire to please. She began to feel she had been ungracious, and straightway adopted a more cordial tone.

"I am sure you mean well, Miss Von Taer," she hastened to say, "and I assure you I am not ungrateful. But it occurred to me we could have nothing in common."

"Oh, my dear! You wrong us both."

"Do you know my uncle?" enquired Beth.

"He is the friend of my father, Mr. Hedrik Von Taer. Our family owes Mr. John Merrick much consideration. Therefore I decided to seek pleasure in the acquaintance of his nieces."

The words and tone seemed alike candid. Beth began to relent. She sat down for the first time, taking a chair opposite Diana.

"You see," she said, artlessly, "I have no personal inclination for society, which is doubtless so large a part of your own amusement. It seems to me artificial and insipid."

"Those who view from a distance the husk of a cocoanut, have little idea of the milk within," declared Diana, softly.

"True," answered Beth. "But I've cracked cocoanuts, and sometimes found the milk sour and tainted."

"The difference you observe in cocoanuts is to be found in the various grades of society. These are not all insipid and artificial, I assure you."

49

"They may be worse," remarked Beth. "I've heard strange tales of your orgies."

Diana was really amused. This girl was proving more interesting than the first niece she had interviewed. Unaccustomed to seeking acquaintances outside her own exclusive circle, and under such circumstances, these meetings were to her in the nature of an adventure. A creature of powerful likes and dislikes, she already hated Beth most heartily; but for that very reason she insisted on cultivating her further acquaintance.

"You must not judge society by the mad pranks of a few of its members," she responded, in her most agreeable manner. "If we are not to set an example in decorum to the rest of the world we are surely unfitted to occupy the high place accorded us. But you must see and decide for yourself."

"I? No, indeed!"

"Ah, do not decide hastily, my dear. Let me become your sponsor for a short time, until you really discover what society is like. Then you may act upon more mature judgment."

"I do not understand you, Miss Von Taer."

"Then I will be more explicit. I am to receive a few friends at my home on the evening of the nineteenth; will you be my guest?"

Beth was puzzled how to answer. The thought crossed her mind that perhaps Uncle John would like her to be courteous to his friend's daughter, and that argument decided her. She accepted the invitation.

"I want you to receive with me," continued Diana, rising. "In that way I shall be able to introduce you to my friends."

Beth wondered at this condescension, but consented to receive. She was annoyed to think how completely she had surrendered to the will of Miss Von Taer, for whom she had conceived the same aversion she had for a snake. She estimated Diana, society belle though she was, to be sly, calculating and deceitful. Worse than all, she was decidedly clever, and therefore dangerous. Nothing good could come of an acquaintance with her, Beth was sure; yet she had pledged herself to meet her and her friends the nineteenth, at a formal society function. How much Beth

De Graf misjudged Diana Von Taer the future will determine.

The interview had tired Diana. As she re-entered her carriage she was undecided whether to go home or hunt up the third niece. But Willing Square was not five minutes' drive from here, so she ordered the coachman to proceed there.

"I am positively out of my element in this affair," she told herself, "for it is more difficult to cultivate these inexperienced girls than I had thought. They are not exactly impossible, as I at first feared, but they are so wholly unconventional as to be somewhat embarrassing as *protégées*. Analyzing the two I have met—the majority—one strikes me as being transparently affected and the other a stubborn, attractive fool. They are equally untrained in diplomacy and unable to cover their real feelings. Here am I, practically dragging them into the limelight, when it would be far better for themselves—perhaps for me—that they remained in oblivion. Ah, well; I called it an adventure; let me hope some tangible plot will develop to compensate me for my trouble. Life seems deadly dull; I need excitement. Is it to be furnished by John Merrick's nieces, I wonder?"

Willing Square is a new district, crowded with fashionable apartment houses. That is, they are called fashionable by their builders and owners and accepted as such by their would-be fashionable occupants. Diana knew at least two good families resident in Willing Square, and though she smiled grimly at the rows of "oppressively new and vulgar" buildings, she still was not ashamed to have her equipage seen waiting there.

Number 3708 Willing Square is a very substantial and cozy appearing apartment building owned in fee by Miss Patricia Doyle. Diana was unaware of this fact, but rang the Doyle bell and ascended to the second floor.

A maid received her with the announcement that Miss Doyle had "just stepped out," but was somewhere in the building. Would the visitor care to wait a few minutes?

Yes; Diana decided she would wait. She took a seat in the smug front parlor and from her position noted the series of rooms that opened one into another throughout the suite, all richly but tastefully furnished in homely, unassuming manner.

"This is better," she mused. "There is no attempt at foolish display in this establishment, at any rate. I hope to find Miss Doyle a sensible, refined person. The name is Irish."

A door slammed somewhere down the line of rooms and a high-pitched voice cried in excited tones:

"I've found a baby! Hi, there, Nunkie, dear —I've found a baby!"

Thereupon came the sound of a chair being pushed back as a man's voice answered in equal glee:

"Why, Patsy, Patsy! it's the little rogue from upstairs. Here, Bobby; come to your own old Uncle!"

"He won't. He belongs to me; don't you, Bobby darlin'?"

A babyish voice babbled merrily, but the sounds were all "goos" and "ahs" without any resemblance to words. Bobby may have imagined he was talking, but he was not very intelligible.

"See here, Patsy Doyle; you gimme that baby," cried the man, pleadingly.

"I found him myself, and he's mine. I've dragged him here all the way from his home upstairs, an' don't you dare lay a finger on him, Uncle John!"

"Fair play, Patsy! Bobby's my chum, and—"

"Well, I'll let you have half of him, Nunkie. Down on your hands and knees, sir, and be a horse. That's it— Now, Bobby, straddle Uncle John and drive him by his necktie—here it is. S-t-e-a-d-y, Uncle; and neigh—neigh like a horse!"

"How does a horse neigh, Patsy?" asked a muffled voice, choking and chuckling at the same time.

" 'Nee, hee-hee—hee, hee!' "

Uncle John tried to neigh, and made a sorry mess of it, although Bobby shrieked with delight.

Then came a sudden hush. Diana caught the maid's voice, perhaps announcing the presence of a visitor, for Patsy cried in subdued accents:

"Goodness me, Mary! why did n't you say so? Listen, Uncle John—"

"Leggo that ear, Bobby—leggo!"

"—You watch the baby, Uncle John, and don't let anything happen to him. I've got a caller."

Diana smiled, a bit scornfully, and then composed her features as a young girl bustled into the room and came toward her with frank cordiality indicated in the wide smile and outstretched hand.

"Pardon my keeping you waiting," said Patsy, dropping into a chair opposite her visitor. "Uncle John and I were romping with the baby from upstairs—Bobby's such a dear! I did n't quite catch the name Mary gave me and forgot to look at your card."

"I am Miss Von Taer."

"Not Diana Von Taer, the swell society girl?" cried Patsy eagerly.

Diana could n't remember when she had been so completely nonplused before. After an involuntary gasp she answered quietly:

"I am Diana Von Taer."

"Well, I'm glad to meet you, just the same," said Patsy, cheerfully. "We outsiders are liable to look on society folk as we would on a cage of monkeys—because we're so very ignorant, you know, and the bars are really between us."

This frank disdain verged on rudeness, although the girl had no intention of being rude. Diana was annoyed in spite of her desire to be tolerant.

"Perhaps the bars are imaginary," she rejoined, carelessly, "and it may be you've been looking at the side-show and not at the entertainment in the main tent. Will you admit that possibility, Miss Doyle?"

Patsy laughed gleefully.

"I think you have me there, Miss Von Taer. And what do *I* know about society? Just nothing at all. It's out of my line entirely."

"Perhaps it is," was the slow response. "Society appeals to only those whose tastes seem to require it."

"And are n't we drawing distinctions?" enquired Miss Doyle. "Society at large is the main evidence of civilization, and all decent folk are members of it."

"Is n't that communism?" asked Diana.

"Perhaps so. It's society at large. But certain classes have leagued together and excluded themselves from their fellows, admitting only those of their own ilk. The people did n't put them on their pedestals—they put themselves there. Yet the people bow down and worship these social gods and seem glad to have them. The newspapers print their pictures and the color of their gowns and how they do their hair and what they eat and what they do, and the poor washwomen and shop-girls and their like read these accounts more religiously than they do their bibles. My maid Mary's a good girl, but she grabs the society sheet of the Sunday paper and reads it from top to bottom. I never look at it myself."

Diana's cheeks were burning. She naturally resented such ridicule, having been born to regard social distinction with awe and reverence. Inwardly resolving to make Miss Patricia Doyle regret the speech she hid all annoyance under her admirable self-control and answered with smooth complacency:

"Your estimate of society, my dear Miss Doyle, is superficial."

"Don't I know it, then?" exclaimed Patsy.

"Culture and breeding, similarity of taste and intellectual pursuits will always attract certain people and band them together in those cliques which are called 'social sets.' They are not secret societies; they have no rules of exclusion; congenial minds are ever welcome to their ranks. This is a natural coalition, in no way artificial. Can you not appreciate that, Miss Doyle?"

"Yes, indeed," admitted Patsy, promptly. "You're quite right, and I'm just one of those stupid creatures who criticise the sun because there's a cloud before it. Probably there are all grades of society, because there are all grades of people."

"I thought you would agree with me when you understood," murmured Diana, and her expression was so smug and satisfied that Patsy was seized with an irresistible spirit of mischief.

"And have n't I seen your own pictures in the Sunday papers?" she asked.

"Perhaps; if you robbed your maid of her pleasure."

"And very pretty pictures they were, too. They

showed culture and breeding all right, and the latest style in gowns. Of course those intellectual high-brows in your set did n't need an introduction to you; you were advertised as an example of ultra-fashionable perfection, to spur the ambition of those lower down in the social scale. Perhaps it's a good thing."

"Are you trying to annoy me?" demanded Diana, her eyes glaring under their curling lashes.

"Dear me—dear me!" cried Patsy, distressed, "see how saucy and impudent I've been—and I did n't mean a bit of it! Won't you forgive me, please, Miss Von Taer? There! we'll begin all over again, and I'll be on my good behavior. I'm so very ignorant, you know!"

Diana smiled at this; it would be folly to show resentment to such a childish creature.

"Unfortunately," she said, "I have been unable to escape the vulgar publicity thrust upon me by the newspapers. The reporters are preying vultures, rapacious for sensation, and have small respect for anyone. I am sure we discourage them as much as we can. I used to weep with mortification when I found myself 'written up';

now, however, I have learned to bear such trials with fortitude—if not with resignation."

"Forgive me!" said Patsy, contritely. "Somehow I've had a false idea of these things. If I knew you better, Miss Von Taer, you'd soon convert me to be an admirer of society."

"I'd like to do that, Miss Doyle, for you interest me. Will you return my call?"

"Indeed I will," promised the girl, readily. "I'm flattered that you called on me at all, Miss Von Taer, for you might easily have amused yourself better. You must be very busy, with all the demands society makes on one. When shall I come? Make it some off time, when we won't be disturbed."

Diana smiled at her eagerness. How nescient the poor little thing was!

"Your cousins, Miss Merrick and Miss De Graf, have consented to receive with me on the evening of the nineteenth. Will you not join us?"

"Louise and Beth!" cried Patsy, astounded.

"Isn't it nice of them? And may I count upon you, also?"

Patsy smiled dubiously into the other's face.

"Let me out of it!" she said. "Can't you see I'm no butterfly?"

Diana saw many things, having taken a shrewd account of the girl long before this. Miss Patricia Doyle was short and plump, with a round, merry face covered with freckles, hair indisputably red and a *retroussé* nose. Also she possessed a pair of wonderful blue eyes—eyes that danced and scintillated with joyous good humor—eyes so captivating that few ever looked beyond them or noted the plain face they glorified. But the critic admitted that the face was charmingly expressive, the sweet and sensitive mouth always in sympathy with the twinkling, candid eyes. Life and energy radiated from her small person, which Miss Von Taer grudgingly conceded to possess unusual fascination. Here was a creature quite imperfect in detail, yet destined to allure and enchant whomsoever she might meet. All this was quite the reverse of Diana's own frigid personality. Patsy would make an excellent foil for her.

"As you please, my dear," she said graciously; "but do you not think it would amuse you to make

your debut in society—unimpeachable society—
and be properly introduced to the occupants of the
'pedestals,' as your cousins will be?"

Patsy reflected. If Beth and Louise had determined to undertake this venture why should she
hold back? Moreover, she experienced a girlish
and wholly natural curiosity to witness a fashionable gathering and "size up" the lions for herself. So she said:

"I'll come, if you really want me; and I'll try
my best to behave nicely. But I can't imagine
why you have chosen to take us three girls under
your wing; unless—" with sudden intuition,
"it's for Uncle John's sake."

"That was it, at first," replied Diana, rising to
go; "but now that I've seen you I'm delighted to
have you on your own account. Come early,
dear; we must be ready to receive our guests by
nine."

"Nine o'clock!" reflected Patsy, when her
visitor had gone; "why, I'm often in bed by that
time."

CHAPTER V

PREPARING FOR THE PLUNGE

John Merrick lived with the Doyles at their Willing Square apartments. There were but two of the Doyles—Patricia and her father, Major Doyle, a tall, handsome, soldierly man with white moustache and hair. The Major was noted as a "character," a keen wit and a most agreeable type of the "old Irish gentleman." He fairly worshipped his daughter, and no one blamed him for it. His business, as special agent and manager for his brother-in-law's millions, kept the Major closely occupied and afforded John Merrick opportunity to spend his days as he pleased. The rich man was supposed to be "retired," yet the care of his investments and income was no light task, as the Major found.

We are accustomed to regard extreme wealth as the result of hard-headed shrewdness, not wholly divorced from unscrupulous methods, yet no one could accuse John Merrick or his representative with being other than kindly, simple-hearted and honest. Uncle John says that he never intended to "get rich"; it was all the result of carelessness. He had been so immersed in business that he failed to notice how fast his fortune was growing. When he awoke to a realization of his immense accumulation he promptly retired, appointing Major Doyle to look after his investments and seeking personal leisure after many years of hard work. He instructed his agent to keep his income from growing into more capital by rendering wise assistance to all worthy charities and individuals, and this, as you may suppose, the Major found a herculean task. Often he denounced Uncle John for refusing to advise him, claiming that the millionaire had selfishly thrust the burden of his wealth on the Major's broad shoulders. While there was an element of truth in this the burden was not so heavy as to make the old soldier unhappy, and the two men loved and respected one another with manly cordiality.

Patricia was recognized as Uncle John's fa-

vorite niece and it was understood she was to inherit the bulk of his property, although some millions might be divided between Beth and Louise
"if they married wisely." Neither Uncle John
nor the Major ever seemed to consider Patsy's
marrying; she was such a child that wedlock for
her seemed a remote possibility.

The Sunday afternoon following Diana Von
Taer's visit to the three nieces found the girls all
congregated in Patsy's own room, where an earnest discussion was being conducted. That left
Uncle John to take his after-dinner nap in the big
Morris chair in the living room, where Major
Doyle sat smoking sulkily while he gazed from the
window and begrudged the moments Patsy was
being kept from him.

Finally the door opened and the three girls
trooped out.

"Huh! Is the conspiracy all cut-an'-dried?"
growled the Major.

Uncle John woke up with a final snort, removed
the newspaper from his face and sat up. He
smiled benignantly upon his nieces.

"It's all your fault, sor!" declared Major Doyle,

selecting the little millionaire as the safest re-
cipient of his displeasure. "Your foolishness has
involved us all in this dreadful complication.
Why on earth could n't you leave well-enough
alone?"

Uncle John received the broadside with tolerant
equanimity.

"What's wrong, my dears?" he enquired, di-
recting his mild glance toward the bevy of young
girls.

"I am unaware that anything is wrong, Uncle,"
replied Louise gravely. "But since we are about
to make our debut in society it is natural we
should have many things to discuss that would
prove quite uninteresting to men. Really, Uncle
John, this is a great event—perhaps the most important event of our lives."

"Shucks an' shoestrings!" grunted the Major.
"What's in this paper-shelled, painted, hollow
thing ye call 'society' to interest three healthy,
wide-awake girls? Tell me that!"

"You don't understand, dear," said Patsy,
soothing him with a kiss.

I think he does," remarked Beth, with meditative brows. "Modern society is a man-made—or woman-made—condition, to a large extent artificial, selfish and unwholesome."

"Oh, Beth!" protested Louise. "You're talking like a rank socialist. I can understand common people sneering at society, which is so far out of their reach; but a girl about to be accepted in the best circles has no right to rail at her own caste."

"There can be no caste in America," declared Beth, stubbornly.

"But there *is* caste in America, and will be so long as the exclusiveness of society is recognized by the people at large," continued Louise. "If it is a 'man-made condition' is n't it the most respected, most refined, most desirable condition that one may attain to?"

"There are plenty of honest and happy people in the world who ignore society altogether," answered Beth. "It strikes me that your social stars are mighty few in the broad firmament of humanity."

"But they're stars, for all that, dear," said Uncle John, smiling at her with a hint of approval in his glance, yet picking up the argument; "and they look mighty big and bright to the crowd below. It's quite natural. You can't keep individuals from gaining distinction, even in America. There are few generals in an army, for instance; and they're 'man-made'; but that's no reason the generals ain't entitled to our admiration."

"Let's admire 'em, then—from a distance," retorted the Major, realizing the military simile was employed to win his sympathy.

"Certain things, my dear Major, are naturally dear to a girl's heart," continued Uncle John, musingly; "and we who are not girls have no right to condemn their natural longings. Girls love dancing, pink teas and fudge-parties, and where can they find 'em in all their perfection but in high society? Girls love admiration and flirtations—you do, my dears; you can't deny it—and the male society swells have the most time to devote to such things. Girls love pretty dresses—"

"Oh, Uncle! you've hit the nail on the head now," exclaimed Patsy, laughing. "We must all have new gowns for this reception, and as we're to assist Miss Von Taer the dresses must har-monize, so to speak, and—and—"

"And be quite suited to the occasion," broke in Louise; "and—"

"And wear our lives out with innumerable fit-tings," concluded Beth, gloomily.

"But why new dresses?" demanded the Major. "You've plenty of old ones that are clean and pretty, I'm sure; and our Patsy had one from the dressmaker only last week that's fit for a queen."

"Oh, Daddy! you don't understand," laughed Patsy.

"This time, Major, I fear you don't," agreed Beth. "Your convictions regarding society may be admirable, but you're weak on the gown ques-tion."

"If the women would only listen to me," began the Major, dictatorially; but Uncle John cut him short.

"They won't, sir; they'll listen to no man when it comes to dressmaking."

"Don't they dress to captivate the men, then?" asked the Major, with fine sarcasm.

"Not at all," answered Louise, loftily. "Men

seldom know what a woman has on, if she looks nice; but women take in every detail of dress and criticise it severely if anything happens to be out of date, ill fitting or in bad taste."

"Then they're in bad taste themselves!" retorted the Major, hotly.

"Tut-tut, sir; who are you to criticise woman's ways?" asked Uncle John, much amused. The Major was silenced, but he glared as if unconvinced.

"Dressmaking is a nuisance," remarked Beth, placidly; "but it's the penalty we pay for being women."

"You're nothing but slips o' girls, not out of your teens," grumbled the Major. And no one paid any attention to him.

"We want to do you credit, Uncle John," said Patsy, brightly. "Perhaps our names will be in the papers."

"They're there already," announced Mr. Merrick, picking up the Sunday paper that lay beside him.

A chorus of exclamations was followed by a dive for the paper, and even the Major smiled grimly as he observed the three girlish heads close together and three pair of eager eyes scanning swiftly the society columns.

"Here it is!" cried Patsy, dancing up and down like a school-girl; and Louise read in a dignified voice—which trembled slightly with excitement and pleasure—the following item:

"Miss Von Taer will receive next Thursday evening at the family mansion in honor of Miss Merrick, Miss Doyle and Miss De Graf. These three charming *debutantes* are nieces of John Merrick, the famous tin-plate magnate."

"Phoo!" growled the Major, during the impressive hush that followed; "that's it, exactly. Your names are printed because you're John Merrick's nieces. If it had n't been for tin-plate, my dears, society never would 'a' known ye at all, at all!"

CHAPTER VI

THE FLY IN THE BROTH

Diana was an experienced entertainer and under her skillful supervision the reception proved eminently successful. Nor had she cause to be ashamed of the three *protégées* she presented to society, since capable *modistes* had supplemented their girlish charms and freshness with costumes pertinent to the occasion. Perhaps Patsy's chubby form looked a little "dumpish" in her party gown, for some of Diana's female guests regarded her with quiet amusement and bored tolerance, while the same critical posse was amazed and envious at Beth's superb beauty and stately bearing. After all, it was Louise who captured the woman contingency and scored the greatest success; for her appearance was not only dainty and attractive but she was so perfectly self-possessed and responsive and bore herself so admirably under the some-

73

what trying circumstances of a debut that she won the cordial goodwill of all whom she encountered.

The hostess was elaborately gowned in white pompadour satin, trimmed with white chiffon and embroidered in pink roses and pearls. The Von Taer home was handsomely decorated for the occasion, since Diana never did anything by halves and for her own credit insisted on attention to those details of display that society recognizes and loves. Hundreds of long-stemmed American Beauties and Kentia palms were combined in beautifying the spacious hall, while orchids in marvelous variety nodded their blossoms in the great drawing-room, where the young ladies received. These rare and precious flowers were arranged in bronze baskets with sprays of maidenhair. In the music room adjoining, great clusters of Madam Chantenay roses embellished the charming scene. Branches of cherry-blossoms, supplied by hothouses, were banked in the lofty dining-room, where a Japanese pergola made of bamboo and lighted with red lanterns was erected at the upper end. The attendants here were Japanese girls in native costume, and the long table was laid with a

lace cloth over pink satin, with butterfly bows of
pink tulle. The table itself was decorated with
cut-glass baskets of Cecil Brunner roses mingled
with lilies of the valley and refreshments were dis-
tributed to the standing guests as they entered.

The affair was in the nature of a typical
"crush," for Diana's list of eligibles included most
of the prominent society folk then in town, and
she was too important a personage to have her in-
vitations disregarded. Beth and Patsy were fairly
bewildered by the numerous introductions, until
names became meaningless in their ears; but
Louise, perfectly composed and in no wise distracted by her surroundings or the music of the
orchestra and the perpetual buzz of conversation
in the crowded rooms, impressed each individual
upon her memory clearly, and was not likely to
blunder in regard to names or individuality in the
future. This is a rare talent, indeed, and scores
largely in one's favor; for no one likes to think
himself so unimportant as to be forgotten, under
any circumstances.

It was during the thick of the reception that one
of Miss Von Taer's intimates, a graceful blond

girl, suddenly seized her arm and whispered: "Oh, Diana! Guess who's here—guess, my dear!"

Diana knew. Her eyes, always narrowed until the lashes shielded their sharp watchfulness, seldom missed observing anything of importance. She pressed her friend's hand and turned again to the line of guests, while Louise, who had overheard the excited whisper, wondered casually what it might mean.

Soon after she knew. A tall, handsome young fellow was bowing before Diana, who—wonder of wonders!—for an instant unclosed her great eyes and shot an electric glance into his smiling face. The glance was brief as unexpected, yet it must have told the young man something, for he flushed and bowed again as if to hide his embarrassment. It also told Louise something, and her heart, which had given a quick bound at sight of the man's face, began to cry out against Diana Von Taer's artifices.

"Mr. Arthur Weldon," said the hostess, in her soft voice; and now, as the young man turned an eager gaze on Louise and half extended his hand, the girl's face grew pale and she imitated Diana to the extent of dropping her eyes and bowing with frigid indifference.

Standing close he whispered "Louise!" in a pleading tone that made Diana frown wickedly. But the girl was unresponsive and another instant forced him to turn to Beth.

"Why, Arthur! are you here, then?" said the girl, in a surprised but cordial tone.

"That is not astonishing, Miss Beth," he replied. "The puzzling fact is that *you* are here— and under such auspices," he added, in a lower tone.

Patsy now claimed him, with a frank greeting, and Arthur Weldon could do little more than press her hand when the line forced him to move on and give place to others.

But this especial young fellow occupied the minds of all four girls long after the crowd had swallowed him up. Diana was uneasy and obviously disturbed by the discovery that he was known to the three cousins, as well as by the memory of his tone as he addressed Louise Merrick. Louise, who had read Diana's quick glance with the accuracy of an intuitionist, felt a sudden suspicion and dislike for Diana now dominating her. Behind all this was a mystery, which shall be explained here because the reader deserves to be more enlightened than the characters themselves.

Arthur Weldon's nature was a queer combination of weakness and strength. He was physically brave but a moral coward. The motherless son of a man wholly immersed in business, he had been much neglected in his youth and his unstable character was largely the result of this neglect. On leaving college he refused a business career planned for him by his father, who cast him off with scornful indifference, and save for a slim temporary allowance promised to disinherit him. It was during this period that Arthur met Louise and fell desperately in love with her. The girl appeared to return the young fellow's devotion, but shrewd, worldly Mrs. Merrick, discovering that the boy was practically disinherited and had no prospects whatever, forbade him the house. Louise, until now but mildly interested in the young man, resented her mother's interference and refused to give him up. She found ways to

meet Arthur Weldon outside her home, so that
the situation had become complicated and dangerous when Uncle John seized his three nieces and
whisked them off to Europe. Young Weldon,
under an assumed name, followed and attached
himself to the party; but John Merrick's suspicions were presently aroused and on discovering
the identity of the youth he forbade him or Louise
to "make love" or even speak of such a thing
during the remainder of the trip.

The young fellow, by manly acts on some occasions and grave weaknesses on others, won Uncle
John's kindly interest. The old gentleman knew
human nature, and saw much to admire as well as
condemn in Louise's friend. Beth and Patsy
found him a pleasant comrade, and after all love-
making was tabooed they were quite a harmonious
party. Finally the sudden death of Weldon's
father left him the possessor of a fortune. He
returned to America to look after his newly-ac-
quired business and became so immersed in it that
Louise felt herself neglected when she came home
expecting him to dance attendance upon her as
before. She treated him coldly and he ceased

calling, his volatile and sensitive nature resenting such treatment.

It is curious what little things influence the trend of human lives. Many estrangements are caused by trifles so intangible that we can scarcely locate them at all.

At first the girl was very unhappy at the alienation, but soon schooled herself to forget her former admirer. Arthur Weldon, for his part, consoled himself by plunging into social distractions and devoting himself to Diana Von Taer, whose strange personality for a time fascinated him.

The business could not hold young Weldon's vacillant temperament for long; neither could Diana. As a matter of fact his heart, more staunch than he himself suspected, had never wavered much from Louise. Yet pride forbade his attempting to renew their former relations. It was now some months since he had seen the girl, and his eager exclamation was wrested from him by surprise and a sudden awakening to the fact that his love for her had merely slumbered.

Diana, worldly, cold and calculating as was her

nature, had been profoundly touched by Arthur's
devotion to her. Usually young men were soon
repulsed by her unfortunate personality, which
was not easily understood. Therefore her intense
nature responded freely to this admirer's attentions, and if Diana could really love she loved
Arthur Weldon. He had never proposed to her
or even intimated it was his intention to do so, but
she conceived a powerful desire to win him and
had never abandoned this motive when he grew
cold and appeared to desert her. Just now he was
recently back from Italy, where he had passed
several months, and Diana's reception was his
first reappearance in society. The girl had
planned to bring him to her side this evening and
intended to exert her strongest fascinations to
lure him back to his former allegiance; so her
annoyance may be guessed when she found her
three *protégées* seemingly more familiar with the
young man than was she herself.

At last the line ended and the introductions
were complete. The *debutantes* were at once the
center of interested groups composed of those who
felt it a duty or pleasure to show them attention.

Diana wandered to the music room and waylaid Arthur Weldon, who was just about to make his escape from the house, having decided it was impossible to find an opportunity to converse with Louise that evening.

"I'm so glad you came, Arthur," she said, a quick glance assuring her they were not overheard. "You landed from the steamer but yesterday, I hear."

"And came straightway to pay my respects to my old friend," he answered lightly. "Isn't it unusual for you to present *debutantes*, Diana?"

"You know these girls, don't you, Arthur?"

"Yes; I met them in Europe."

"And flirted with Miss Merrick? Be honest, Arthur. I know your secret."

"Do you? Then you know we were merely good friends," said he, annoyed at her accusation.

"Of course. You called her 'Louise,' did n't you?"

"To be sure. And Patsy called me 'Arthur.' You may have heard her."

"Patsy?"

"That's Miss Patricia Doyle—our dear little Patsy."

"Oh. I'm sure you did n't fall in love with *her*, at any rate."

"I'm not so sure. Everybody loves Patsy. But I had no time for love-making. I was doing Europe."

"Was n't that a year or so ago?" she asked, realizing he was trying to evade further reference to Louise.

"Yes."

"And since then?"

"I've been away the last six or seven months, as you know, on my second trip abroad."

"But before that—when you first returned?"

"If I remember rightly I was then much in the society of Miss Von Taer. Is the catechism ended at last?"

"Yes," she replied, laughing. "Don't think me inquisitive, Arthur; I was surprised to find you knew these girls, with whom I am myself but slightly acquainted."

"Yet you introduce them to your very select set?"

"To please my father, who wishes to please Mr. Merrick."

"I understand," said he, nodding. "But they're nice girls, Diana. You're not running chances, I assure you."

"That relieves me," she replied rather scornfully. "If Arthur Weldon will vouch for them—"

"But I don't. I'll vouch for no one—not even myself," he declared hastily. She was calmly reading his face, and did not seem to approve the text.

"Are you as fickle as ever, then, *mon cher?*" she asked, softly.

"I'm not fickle, Diana. My fault is that I'm never serious."

"Never?"

"I cannot remember ever being serious; at least, where a girl was concerned."

Diana bit her lips to restrain a frown, but her eyes, which he was avoiding, flashed wickedly.

"That is surely a fault, my Arthur," was her tender reply. "Were you never serious during our quiet evenings together; our dances, theatre parties and romps?"

"That was merely fun. And you, Diana?"

"Oh, I enjoyed the fun, too. It meant so much to me. I began to live, then, and found life very sweet. But when you suddenly left me and went abroad—ah, *that* was indeed serious."

Her tone was full of passionate yearning. He laughed, trying to appear at ease. Some sort of an understanding must be had with Diana sooner or later, and she might as well realize at this present interview that the old relations could not be restored. His nature was not brutal and he disliked to hurt her; moreover, the boy had an uneasy feeling that he had been a far more ardent admirer of this peculiar girl than any fellow should be who had had no serious intentions; yet it would be folly to allow Diana to think she could win him back to his former allegiance. No compromising word had ever left his lips; he had never spoken of love to her. Yet the girl's attitude seemed to infer a certain possession of him which was far from agreeable.

Having gone so far, he should have said more; but here again his lack of moral courage proved his stumbling-block, and he weakly evaded a frank expression of his true feelings.

"Life," he began somewhat haltingly, to break the embarrassing pause, "is only serious when we make it so; and as soon as we make it serious it makes us unhappy. So I've adopted one invariable rule: to laugh and be gay."

"Then I too will be gay, and together we'll enjoy life," responded Diana, with an effort to speak lightly. "I shall let your moods be my moods, Arthur, as a good friend should. Are we not affinities?"

Again he knew not what to say. Her persistence in clinging to her intangible hold upon him was extremely irritating, and he realized the girl was far too clever for him to cope with and was liable to cause him future trouble. Instead of seizing the opportunity to frankly undeceive her he foolishly evaded the subject.

"You've been tempting fate to-night," he remarked with assumed carelessness. "Don't you remember that to stand four girls in a row is a bad omen?"

"Only for the one who first winks. Is n't that

the way the saying goes? I seldom wink, myself," she continued, smilingly. "But I have no faith in ill omens. Their power is entirely due to mental fear."

"I think not," said Arthur, glad the conversation had taken this turn. "Once I knew a fellow with thirteen letters in his name. He had no mental fear. But he proposed to a girl—and was accepted."

She gave him one of those sudden, swift glances that were so disconcerting.

"If you had a middle initial, there would be thirteen letters in your own name, Arthur Weldon."

"But I have n't, Diana; I have n't," he protested, eagerly. "And if ever I propose to a girl I'm sure she'll refuse me. But I've no intention of doing such a crazy thing, so I'm perfectly safe."

"You cannot be sure until you try, Arthur," she replied pointedly, and with a start he became conscious that he was again treading upon dangerous ground.

"Come; let us rejoin your guests," said he, offering her his arm. "They would all hate me if they knew I was keeping the fair Diana from them so long."

"Arthur, I must have a good long talk with you—one of our old, delightful confabs," she said, earnestly. "Will you call Sunday afternoon? Then we shall be quite undisturbed."

He hesitated.

"Sunday afternoon?" he answered.

"Yes."

"All right; I'll come, Diana."

She gave him a grateful look and taking his arm allowed him to lead her back to the drawing-room. The crush was over, many having already departed. Some of the young people were dancing in the open spaces to the music of a string orchestra hidden behind a bank of ferns in the hall.

Louise and Beth were the centers of attentive circles; Patsy conversed with merry freedom with a group of ancient dowagers, who delighted in her freshness and healthy vigor and were flattered by her consideration. Mrs. Merrick—for she had been invited—sat in a corner gorgeously robed and stiff as a poker, her eyes devouring the scene. Noting the triumph of Louise she failed to realize she was herself neglected.

A single glance sufficed to acquaint Diana with all this, and after a gracious word to her guests here and there she asked Arthur to dance with her. He could not well refuse, but felt irritated and annoyed when he observed Louise's eyes fastened upon him in amused disdain. After a few turns he discovered some departing ones waiting to bid their hostess *adieu*, and escaped from his unpleasant predicament by halting his partner before them. Then he slipped away and quietly left the house before Diana had time to miss him.

CHAPTER VII

THE HERO ENTERS AND TROUBLE BEGINS

The Von Taer reception fully launched the three nieces in society. Endorsed by Diana and backed by John Merrick's millions and their own winsome charms, they were sure to become favorites in that admirable set to which they had fortunately gained admittance.

Cards poured in upon them during the succeeding days and they found themselves busy returning calls and attending dinners, fêtes, bridge parties and similar diversions. The great Mrs. Sandringham took a decided fancy to Louise, and when the committee was appointed to arrange for the social Kermess to be held in December, this dictatorial leader had the girl's name included in the list. Naturally the favor led to all three cousins taking active part in the most famous social event of the season, and as an especial mark of favoritism they were appointed to conduct the "flower booth," one of the important features of the Kermess.

Mrs. Merrick was in the seventh heaven of ecstatic delight; Uncle John declared his three girls were sure to become shining lights, if not actual constellations, wherever they might be placed; Major Doyle growled and protested; but was secretly pleased to have "our Patsy the captain of the dress parade," where he fondly imagined she outclassed all others. All former denunciations of society at large were now ignored, even by unimpressive Beth, and the girls soon became deeply interested in their novel experiences.

Arthur Weldon sulked at home, unhappy and undecided, for a day or two after the reception. Sunday noon he dispatched a messenger to Diana with a note saying he would be unable to keep his appointment with her that afternoon. Then he went straight to the Merrick home and sent his card to Louise. The girl flushed, smiled, frowned, and decided to go down.

No one had ever interested her so much as Arthur Weldon. There had been a spice of romance about their former relations that made her still regard him as exceptional among mankind. She had been asking herself, since the night of the reception, if she still loved him, but could not come to a positive conclusion. The boy was no longer "ineligible," as he had been at first; even Uncle John could now have no serious objection to him. He was handsome, agreeable, occupied a good social position and was fairly well off in the way of worldly goods—the last point removing Mrs. Merrick's former rejection of Arthur as a desirable son-in-law.

But girls are wayward and peculiar in such an *affaire du cœur,* and none of these things might have weighed with Louise had she not discovered that Diana Von Taer was in love with Arthur and intended to win him. That aroused the girl's fighting instincts, rendered the young man doubly important, and easily caused Louise to forget her resentment at his temporary desertion of her. Perhaps, she reflected, it had partially been her own fault. Now that Arthur showed a disposition to renew their friendship, and she might promise herself the satisfaction of defeating Diana's ambitions, it would be diplomatic, at least, to receive the youth with cordial frankness.

Therefore she greeted him smilingly and with outstretched hand, saying:

"This is quite a surprise, Mr. Weldon. I'd a notion you had forgotten me."

"No, indeed, Louise! How could you imagine such a thing?" he answered, reproachfully.

"There was some evidence of the fact," she asserted archly. "At one time you gave me no peace; then you became retiring. At last you disappeared wholly. What could I think, sir, under such circumstances?"

He stood looking down at her thoughtfully. How pretty she had grown; and how mature and womanly.

"Louise," said he, gently, "don't let us indulge in mutual reproaches. Some one must have been at fault and I'll willingly take all the blame if you will forgive me. Once we were—were good friends. We—we intended to be still more to one another, Louise, but something occurred, I don't know what, to—to separate us."

"Why, you went away," said the girl, laughing; "and that of course separated us."

"You treated me like a beggar; don't forget that part of it, dear. Of course I went away."

"And consoled yourself with a certain Miss

Diana Von Taer. It has lately been rumored you are engaged to her."

"Me? What nonsense?" But he flushed guiltily, and Louise noted everything and determined he should not escape punishment.

"Diana, at least, is in earnest," she remarked, with assumed indifference. "You may not care to deny that you have been very attentive to her."

"Not especially so," he declared, stoutly.

"People gossip, you know. And Diana is charming."

"She's an iceberg!"

"Oh, you have discovered that? Was she wholly unresponsive, then?"

"No," he said, with a touch of anger. "I have never cared for Diana, except in a friendly way. She amused me for a while when—when I was wretched. But I never made love to her; not for a moment. Afterward, why—then——"

"Well; what then?" as he hesitated, growing red again.

"I found she had taken my careless attentions in earnest, and the play was getting dangerous. So I went abroad."

Louise considered this explanation seriously. She believed he was speaking the truth, so far as he knew. But at the same time she realized from her own experience that Arthur might as easily deceive himself as Diana in his estimate as to the warmth of the devotion he displayed. His nature was impetuous and ardent. That Diana should have taken his attentions seriously and become infatuated with the handsome young fellow was not a matter to cause surprise.

Gradually Louise felt her resentment disappearing. In Arthur's presence the charm of his personality influenced her to be lenient with his shortcomings. And his evident desire for a reconciliation found an echo in her own heart.

Mutual explanations are excellent to clear a murky atmosphere, and an hour's earnest conversation did much to restore these two congenial spirits to their former affectionate relations. Of course Louise did not succumb too fully to his pleadings, for her feminine instinct warned her to keep the boy on "the anxious seat" long enough to enable him to appreciate her value and the honor of winning her good graces. Moreover, she made some severe conditions and put him on his good behavior. If he proved worthy, and was steadfast and true, why then the future might reward him freely.

Diana had been making careful plans for her interview with Arthur that Sunday afternoon. With no futile attempt to deceive herself as to existent conditions she coldly weighed the chances in her mental scale and concluded she had sufficient power to win this unstable youth to her side and induce him to forget that such a person as Louise Merrick ever existed.

Diana was little experienced in such affairs, it is true. Arthur Weldon had been her first and only declared admirer, and no one living had studied his peculiar nature more critically than this observant girl. Also she knew well her own physical failings. She realized that her personality was to many repulsive, rather than attractive, and this in spite of her exquisite form, her perfect breeding and many undeniable accomplishments. Men, as a rule, seldom remained at her side save through politeness, and even seemed to fear her; but never until now had she cared for any man sufficiently to wish to retain or interest him. There were unsuspected fascinations lying dormant in her nature, and Miss Von Taer calmly reflected that the exercise of these qualities, backed by her native wit and capacity for intrigue, could easily accomplish the object she desired.

Thus she had planned her campaign and carefully dressed herself in anticipation of Arthur's call when his note came canceling the engagement. After rereading his lame excuse she sat down in a quiet corner and began to think. The first gun had been fired, the battle was on, and like a wise general she carefully marshaled her forces for combat.

An hour or two later she turned to her telephone book and called up the Merrick establishment. A voice, that of a maid, evidently, answered her.

"I wish to speak with Miss Merrick," said Diana.

Louise, annoyed at being disturbed, left Arthur's side to respond to the call.

"Who is it, please?" she asked.

"Is Mr. Weldon still there, or has he gone?"

enquired Diana, disguising her voice and speaking imperatively.

"Why, he's still here," answered bewildered Louise; "but who is talking, please?"

No answer.

"Do you wish to speak with Mr. Weldon?" continued the girl, mystified at such an odd proceedure.

Diana hung up her receiver, severing the connection. The click of the instrument assured Louise there was no use in waiting longer, so she returned to Arthur. She could not even guess who had called her. Arthur could, though, when he had heard her story, and Diana's impudent meddling made him distinctly uneasy. He took care not to enlighten Louise, and the incident was soon forgotten by her.

"It proved just as I expected," mused Diana, huddled in her reclining chair. "The fool has thrown me over to go to her. But this is not important. With the situation so clearly defined I shall know exactly what I must do to protect my own interests."

Mr. Von Taer was away from home that

Sunday afternoon, and would not return until a late hour. Diana went to the telephone again and after several unsuccessful attempts located her cousin, Mr. Charles Connoldy Mershone, at a club.

"It's Diana," she said, when at last communication was established. "I want you to come over and see me; at once."

"You'll have to excuse me, Di," was the answer. "I was unceremoniously kicked out the last time, you know."

"Father's away. It's all right, Charlie. Come along."

"Can't see it, my fair cousin. You've all treated me like a bull-pup, and I'm not anxious to mix up with that sort of a relationship. Anything more? I'm going to play pool to win my dinner."

"Funds running low, Charlie?"

"Worse than that; they're invisible."

"Then pay attention. Call a taxi at once, and get here as soon as you can. I'll foot the bill— and any others that happen to be bothering you."

A low, surprised whistle came over the wire.

"What's up, Di?" he asked, with new interest.

"Come and find out."

"Can I be useful?"

"Assuredly; to yourself."

"All right; I'm on the way."

He hung up, and Diana gave a sigh of content as she slowly returned to her den and the easy chair, where Mr. Mershone found her "coiled" some half hour later.

"This is a queer go," said the young man, taking a seat and glancing around with knitted brows. "It isn't so long since dear Uncle Hedrik tumbled me out of here neck and crop; and now Cousin Diana invites me to return."

At first glance young Mershone seemed an attractive young fellow, tall, finely formed and well groomed. But his eyes were too close together and his handsome features bore unmistakable marks of dissipation.

"You disgraced us a year or so ago, Charlie," said Diana, in her soft, quiet accents, "and under such circumstances we could not tolerate you. You can scarcely blame us for cutting your acquaintance. But now—"

"Well, now?" he enquired coolly, trying to read her impassive face.

"I need the services of just such an unscrupulous and clever individual as you have proven yourself to be. I'm willing to pay liberally for those services, and you doubtless need the money. Are we allies, then?"

Mershone laughed, with little genuine mirth.

"Of course, my dear cousin," he responded; "provided you propose any legal villainy. I'm not partial to the police; but I really need the money, as you suggest."

"And you will be faithful?" she asked, regarding him doubtfully.

"To the cause, you may be sure. But understand me: I balk at murder and burglary. Somehow, the police seem to know me. I'll not do anything that might lead to a jail sentence, because there are easier ways to get money. However, I don't imagine your proposed plan is very desperate, Diana; it's more liable to be dirty work. Never mind; you may command me, my dear cousin—if the pay is ample."

"The pay will be ample if you succeed," she began.

"I don't like that. I may not succeed."

"Listen to me, Charlie. Do you know Arthur Weldon?"

"Slightly; not very well."

"I intend to marry him. He has paid me marked attentions in the past; but now—he—"

"Wants to slip the leash. Quite natural, my dear."

"He has become infatuated with another girl; a light-headed, inexperienced little thing who is likely to marry the first man who asks her. She is very rich—in her own right, too—and her husband will be a fortunate man."

Mershone stared at her. Then he whistled, took a few turns up and down the room, and reseated himself.

"Evidently!" he ejaculated, lighting a cigarette without permission and then leaning back thoughtfully in his chair.

"Charlie," continued Diana, "you may as well marry Louise Merrick and settle down to a life of respectability. You've a dashing, masterful way which no girl of her sort can long resist. I propose that you make desperate love to Louise Merrick and so cut Arthur Weldon out of the deal entirely. My part of the comedy will be to attract him to my side again. Now you have the entire proposition in a nutshell."

He smoked for a time in reflective silence.

"What's the girl like?" he enquired, presently. "Is she attractive?"

"Sufficiently so to fascinate Arthur Weldon. Moreover, she has just been introduced in our set, and knows nothing of your shady past history. Even if rumors came to her ears, young creatures of her sort often find a subtle charm in a man accused of being 'naughty.'"

"Humph!"

"If you win her, you get a wife easily managed and a splendid fortune to squander as you please."

"Sounds interesting, Di, does n't it? But—"

"In regard to preliminary expenses," she interrupted, calmly, "I have said that your reward will be ample when you have won the game. But meantime I am willing to invest the necessary funds in the enterprise. I will allow you a thousand a month."

"Bah! that's nothing at all!" said he, contemptuously, as he flicked the ashes from his cigarette.

"What do you demand, then?"

"Five hundred a week, in advance. It's an expensive job, Di."

"Very well; I will give you five hundred a week; but only as long as you work earnestly to carry out the plot. I shall watch you, Charlie. And you must not lose sight of the ultimate reward."

"I won't, my sweet cousin. It's a bargain," he said, readily enough. "When do I begin, and what's the program?"

"Draw your chair nearer," said Diana, restraining her triumphant joy. "I'll explain everything to you in detail. It will be my part to plan, and yours to execute."

"Good!" he exclaimed, with a cheerful grin. "I feel like an executioner already!"

CHAPTER VIII

OPENING THE CAMPAIGN

Louise's little romance, which now began to thrive vigorously, was regarded with calmness by her cousins and her mother, who knew of the former episode between her and Arthur and attached little importance to the renewed flirtation in which they indulged. That they were deceived in their estimate was due to the girl's reputation for frivolity where young men were concerned. She had been dubbed a "flirt" ever since she first began to wear long dresses, and her nature was not considered deep enough for her heart to be ever seriously affected. Therefore the young girl was gravely misjudged.

Louise was not one to bare her heart, even to her most intimate friends, and no one now suspected that at last her deepest, truest womanly affections were seriously involved. The love for

Arthur that had lain dormant in her heart was aroused at a time when she was more mature and capable of recognizing truly her feelings, so that it was not long before she surrendered her reserve and admitted to him that life would mean little for her unless they might pass the years together. For his part, young Weldon sincerely loved Louise, and had never wavered from his firm devotion during all the past months of misunderstanding.

The general impression that they were "merely flirting" afforded the lovers ample opportunity to have their walks and drives together undisturbed, and during these soulful communions they arrived at such a perfect understanding that both were confident nothing could ever disturb their trust and confidence.

It was at a theatre party that the three *debutantes* first met Charlie Mershone, but they saw little of him that first evening and scarcely noticed his presence. Louise, indeed, noted that his eyes were fixed upon her more than once with thinly veiled admiration, and without a thought of disloyalty to Arthur, but acting upon the impulse of her coquettish nature, she responded with a demure smile of encouragement.

Charlie Mershone was an adept at playing parts. He at first regarded Louise much as a hunter does the game he is stalking. Patsy Doyle was more jolly and Beth De Graf more beautiful than Miss Merrick; but the young man would in any event have preferred the latter's dainty personality. When he found her responsive to his admiring glances he was astounded to note his heart beating rapidly—a thing quite foreign to his usual temperament. Yes, this girl would do very nicely, both as a wife and as a banker. Assuredly the game was well worth playing, as Diana had asserted. He must make it his business to discover what difficulties must be overcome in winning her. Of course Arthur Weldon was the main stumbling-block; but Weldon was a ninny; he must be thrust aside; Diana had promised to attend to that.

Never in his life had Charles Connoldy Mershone been in earnest before. After his first interview with Louise Merrick he became in deadly earnest. His second meeting with her was at

Marie Delmar's bridge-whist party, where they had opportunity for an extended conversation. Arthur was present this evening, but by some chance Mershone drew Louise for his partner at cards, and being a skillful player he carried her in progression from table to table, leaving poor Arthur far behind and indulging in merry repartee and mild flirtation until they felt they were quite well acquainted.

Louise found the young man a charming conversationalist. He had a dashing, confidential way of addressing the girl which impressed her as flattering and agreeable, while his spirits were so exuberant and sparkling with humor that she was thoroughly amused every moment while in his society. Indeed, Mr. Mershone was really talented, and had he possessed any manly attributes, or even the ordinary honorable instincts of mankind, there is little doubt he would have been a popular favorite. But he had made his mark, and it was a rather grimy one. From earliest youth he had been guilty of discreditable acts that had won for him the contempt of all right-minded people. That he was still accepted with lax toler-

ance by some of the more thoughtless matrons
of the fashionable set was due to his family name.
They could not forget that in spite of his numerous lapses from respectability he was still a Mershone. Not one of the careless mothers who admitted him to her house would have allowed her
daughter to wed him, and the degree of tolerance
extended to him was fully appreciated by Mershone himself. He knew he was practically barred
from the most desirable circles and seldom im-
posed himself upon his former acquaintances; but
now, with a distinct object in view, he callously
disregarded the doubtful looks he encountered
and showed himself in every drawing-room where
he could secure an invitation or impudently in-
trude himself. He made frank avowals that he
had "reformed" and abandoned his evil ways
forever. Some there were who accepted this
statement seriously, and Diana furthered his cause
by treating him graciously whenever they met,
whereas she had formerly refused to recognize
her cousin.

Louise knew nothing at all of Charlie Mershone's history and permitted him to call when

he eagerly requested the favor; but on the way
home from the Delmars Arthur, who had glowered at the usurper all the evening, took pains
to hint to Louise that Mershone was an undesir-
able acquaintance and had a bad record. Of
course she laughed at him and teased him, thinking he was jealous and rejoicing that in Mershone she had a tool to "keep Arthur toeing the
mark." As a matter of truth she had really
missed her lover's companionship that evening,
but forbore to apprise him of the fact.

And now the great Kermess began to occupy
the minds of the three cousins, who were to share
the important "Flower Booth" between them.
The Kermess was to be the holiday sensation of
the season and bade fair to eclipse the horse show
in popularity. It was primarily a charitable entertainment, as the net receipts were to be divided
among several deserving hospitals; nevertheless
it was classed as a high society function and only
the elect were to take active part in the affair.

The ball room at the Waldorf had been secured
and many splendid booths were to be erected for
the sale of novelties, notions and refreshments.

There were to be lotteries and auctions, national dances given by groups of society belles, and other novel entertainments calculated to empty the pockets of the unwary.

Beth was somewhat indignant to find that she and her cousins, having been assigned to the flower booth, were expected to erect a pavilion and decorate it at their own expense, as well as to provide the stock of flowers to be sold. "There is no fund for preliminary expenses, you know," remarked Mrs. Sandringham, "and of course all the receipts are to go to charity; so there is nothing to do but stand these little bills ourselves. We all do it willingly. The papers make a good deal of the Kermess, and the advertisement we get is worth all it costs us."

Beth did not see the force of this argument. She thought it was dreadful for society—really good society—to wish to advertise itself; but gradually she was learning that this was merely a part of the game. To be talked about, to have her goings and comings heralded in the society columns and her gowns described on every possible occasion, seemed the desire of every society woman, and she who could show the biggest scrap-book of clippings was considered of highest importance.

Uncle John laughed joyously when told that the expenses of the flower booth would fall on the shoulders of his girls and there was no later recompense.

"Why not?" he cried. "Must n't we pay the fiddler if we dance?"

"It's a hold-up game," declared Beth, angrily. "I'll have nothing to do with it."

"Yes, you will, my dear," replied her uncle; "and to avoid separating you chicks from your pin-money I'm going to stand every cent of the expense myself. Why, it's for charity, is n't it? Charity covers a multitude of sins, and I'm just a miserable sinner that needs a bath-robe to snuggle in. How can the poor be better served than by robbing the rich? Go ahead, girls, and rig up the swellest booth that money will build. I'll furnish as many flowers as you can sell, and charity ought to get a neat little nest-egg out of the deal."

"That's nice of you," said Patsy, kissing him; "but it's an imposition, all the same."

"It's a blessing, my dear. It will help a bit to ease off that dreadful income that threatens to crush me," he rejoined, smiling at them. And the nieces made no further protest, well knowing the kindly old gentleman would derive untold pleasure in carrying out his generous plans.

The flower booth, designed by a famous architect, proved a splendid and most imposing structure. It was capped by a monster bouquet of artificial orchids in *papier-maché*, which reached twenty feet into the air. The three cousins had their gowns especially designed for the occasion. Beth represented a lily, Louise a Gold-of-Ophir rose, and Patricia a pansy.

The big ball room had been turned over to the society people several days in advance, that the elaborate preparations might be completed in time, and during this period groups of busy, energetic young folks gathered by day and in the evenings, decorating, flirting, rehearsing the fancy dances, and amusing themselves generally.

Arthur Weldon was there to assist Uncle John's nieces; but his pleasure was somewhat marred by the persistent presence of Charlie Mershone, who, having called once or twice upon Louise, felt at liberty to attach himself to her party. The ferocious looks of his rival were ignored by this designing young man and he had no hesitation in interrupting a *tete-à-tête* to monopolize the girl for himself.

Louise was amused, thinking it fun to worry Arthur by flirting mildly with Mr. Mershone, for whom she cared not a jot. Both Patsy and Beth took occasion to remonstrate with her for this folly, for having known Weldon for a long time and journeyed with him through a part of Europe, they naturally espoused his cause, liking him as much as they intuitively disliked Mershone.

One evening Arthur, his patience well-nigh exhausted, talked seriously with Louise.

"This fellow Mershone," said he, "is a bad egg, a despicable son of a decadent family. His mother was Hedrik Von Taer's sister, but the poor thing has been dead many years. Not long ago Charlie was tabooed by even the rather fast set he belonged to, and the Von Taers, especially, refused to recognize their relative. Now he seems to go everywhere again. I don't know what has caused the change, I'm sure."

"Why, he has reformed," declared Louise; "Diana told me so. She said he had been a bit wild, as all young men are; but now his behavior is irreproachable."

"I don't believe a word of it," insisted Arthur. "Mershone is a natural cad; he's been guilty of all sorts of dirty tricks, and is capable of many more. If you'll watch out, Louise, you'll see that all the girls are shy of being found in his society, and all the chaperones cluck to their fledglings the moment the hawk appears. You're a novice in society just yet, my dear, and it won't do you any good to encourage Charlie Mershone, whom everyone else avoids."

"He's very nice," returned Louise, lightly.

"Yes; he must be nicer than I am," admitted the young man, glumly, and thereupon he became silent and morose and Louise found her evening spoiled.

The warning did not fall on barren ground, however. In the seclusion of her own room the girl thought it all over and decided she had teased her true lover enough. Arthur had not scolded or reproached her, despite his annoyance, and she had a feeling that his judgment of Charlie Mershone was quite right. Although the latter was evidently madly in love with her the girl had the discretion to see how selfish and unrestrained was his nature, and once or twice he had already frightened her by his impetuosity. She decided to retreat cautiously but positively from further association with him, and at once began to show the young man coolness.

Mershone must have been chagrined, but he did not allow Louise to see there was any change in their relations as far as he was concerned. He merely redoubled his attentions, sending her flowers and bonbons daily, accompanied by ardently worded but respectful notes. Really, Louise was in a quandary, and she frankly admitted to Arthur that she had brought this embarassment upon herself. Yet Arthur could do or say little to comfort her. He longed secretly to "punch Mershone's head," but could find no occasion for such decided action.

Diana, during this time, treated both Arthur

and Louise with marked cordiality. Believing her time would come to take part in the comedy she refrained from interfering prematurely with the progress of events. She managed to meet her accomplice at frequent intervals and was pleased that there was no necessity to urge Charlie to do his utmost in separating the lovers.

"I'm bound to win, Di," he said grimly, "for I love the girl even better than I do her fortune. And of one thing you may rest assured; Weldon shall never marry her."

"What will you do?" asked Diana, curiously.

"Anything! Everything that is necessary to accomplish my purpose."

"Be careful," said she warningly. "Keep a cool head, Charlie, and don't do anything foolish. Still—"

"Well?"

"If it is necessary to take a few chances, do it. Arthur Weldon must not marry Louise Merrick!"

CHAPTER IX

THE VON TAER PEARLS

Uncle John really had more fun out of the famous Kermess than anyone else. The preparations gave him something to do, and he enjoyed doing—openly, as well as in secret ways. Having declared that he would stock the flower booth at his own expense, he confided to no one his plans. The girls may have thought he would merely leave orders with a florist; but that was not the Merrick way of doing things. Instead, he visited the most famous greenhouses within a radius of many miles, contracting for all the floral blooms that art and skill could produce. The Kermess was to be a three days' affair, and each day the floral treasures of the east were delivered in reckless profusion at the flower booth, which thus became the center of attraction and the marvel of the public. The girls were delighted to be able to dispense such blooms, and their success as saleswomen was assured at once.

Of course the fair vendors were ignorant of the value of their wares, for Uncle John refused to tell them how extravagant he had been; so they were obliged to guess at the sums to be demanded and in consequence sold priceless orchids and rare hothouse flora at such ridiculous rates that Mr. Merrick chuckled with amusement until he nearly choked.

The public being "cordially invited" Uncle John was present on that first important evening, and —wonder of wonders—was arrayed in an immaculate full-dress suit that fitted his chubby form like the skin of a banana. Mayor Doyle, likewise disguised, locked arms with his brother-in-law and stalked gravely among the throng; but neither ever got to a point in the big room where the flower booth was not in plain sight. The Major's pride in "our Patsy" was something superb; Uncle John was proud of all three of his nieces. As the sale of wares was for the benefit of charity these old fellows purchased liberally—mostly flowers—

and had enough parcels sent home to fill a delivery wagon.

One disagreeable incident, only, marred this otherwise successful evening—successful especially for the three cousins, whose beauty and grace won the hearts of all.

Diana Von Taer was stationed in the "Hindoo Booth," and the oriental costume she wore exactly fitted her sensuous style of beauty. To enhance its effect she had worn around her neck the famous string of Von Taer pearls, a collection said to be unmatched in beauty and unequaled in value in all New York.

The "Hindoo Booth" was near enough to the "Flower Booth" for Diana to watch the cousins, and the triumph of her late *protégées* was very bitter for her to endure. Especially annoying was it to find Arthur Weldon devoting himself assiduously to Louise, who looked charming in her rose gown and favored Arthur in a marked way, although Charlie Mershone, refusing to be ignored, also leaned over the counter of the booth and chatted continually, striving to draw Miss Merrick's attention to himself.

Forced to observe all this, Diana soon lost her accustomed coolness. The sight of the happy faces of Arthur and Louise aroused all the rancor and subtile wit that she possessed, and she resolved upon an act that she would not before have believed herself capable of. Leaning down, she released the catch of the famous pearls and unobserved concealed them in a handkerchief. Then, leaving her booth, she sauntered slowly over to the floral display, which was surrounded for the moment by a crowd of eager customers. Many of the vases and pottery jars which had contained flowers now stood empty, and just before the station of Louise Merrick the stock was sadly depleted. This was, of course, offset by the store of money in the little drawer beside the fair saleslady, and Louise, having greeted Diana with a smile and nod, turned to renew her conversation with the young men besieging her.

Diana leaned gracefully over the counter, resting the hand containing the handkerchief over the mouth of an empty Doulton vase—empty save for the water which had nourished the flowers. At the same time she caught Louise's eye and with a gesture brought the girl to her side.

"Those young men are wealthy," she said, carelessly, her head close to that of Louise. "Make them pay well for their purchases, my dear."

"I can't rob them, Diana," was the laughing rejoinder.

"But it is your duty to rob, at a Kermess, and in the interests of charity," persisted Diana, maintaining her voice at a whisper.

Louise was annoyed.

"Thank you," she said, and went back to the group awaiting her.

The floral booth was triangular. Beth officiated at one of the three sides, Patsy at another, and Louise at the third. Diana now passed softly around the booth, interchanging a word with the other two girls, after which she returned to her own station.

Presently, while chatting with a group of acquaintances, she suddenly clasped her throat and assuming an expression of horror exclaimed:

"My pearls!"

"What, the Von Taer pearls?" cried one.

"The Von Taer pearls," said Diana, as if dazed by her misfortune.

"And you've lost them, dear?"

"They're lost!" she echoed.

Well, there was excitement then, you may be sure. One man hurried to notify the door-keeper and the private detective employed on all such occasions, while others hastily searched the booth —of course in vain. Diana seemed distracted and the news spread quickly through the assemblage.

"Have you left this booth at all?" asked a quiet voice, that of the official whose business it was to investigate.

"I—I merely walked over to the floral booth opposite, and exchanged a word with Miss Merrick, and the others there," she explained.

The search was resumed, and Charlie Mershone sauntered over.

"What's this, Di? Lost the big pearls, I hear," he said.

She took him aside and whispered something to him. He nodded and returned at once to the flower booth, around which a crowd of searchers now gathered, much to the annoyance of Louise and her cousins.

"It's all foolishness, you know," said Uncle John, to the Major, confidentially. "If the girl really dropped her pearls some one has picked them up, long ago."

Young Mershone seemed searching the floral booth as earnestly as the others, and awkwardly knocked the Doulton vase from the shelf with his elbow. It smashed to fragments and in the pool of water on the floor appeared the missing pearls.

There was an awkward silence for a moment, while all eyes turned curiously upon Louise, who served this side of the triangle. The girl appeared turned to stone as she gazed down at the gems. Mershone laughed disagreeably and picked up the recovered treasure, which Diana ran forward and seized.

"H-m-m!" said the detective, with a shrug; "this is a strange occurrence—a very strange occurrence, indeed. Miss Von Taer, do you wish—"

"No!" exclaimed Diana, haughtily. "I accuse no one. It is enough that an accident has restored to me the heirloom."

Stiffly she marched back to her own booth, and the crowd quietly dispersed, leaving only Arthur, Uncle John and the Major standing to support Louise and her astonished cousins.

"Why, confound it!" cried the little millionaire, with a red face, "does the jade mean to insinuate—"

"Not at all, sor," interrupted the Major, sternly; "her early education has been neglected, that's all."

"Come dear," pleaded Arthur to Louise; "let us go home."

"By no means!" announced Beth, positively; "let us stay where we belong. Why, we're not half sold out yet!"

CHAPTER X

MISLED

Arthur Weldon met Mershone at a club next afternoon. "You low scoundrel!" he exclaimed. "It was *your* trick to accuse Miss Merrick of a theft last night."

"Was she accused?" enquired the other, blandly. "I had n't heard, really."

"You did it yourself!"

"Dear me!" said Mershone, deliberately lighting a cigarette.

"You or your precious cousin—you're both alike," declared Arthur, bitterly. "But you **have** given us wisdom, Mershone. We'll see you don't trick us again."

The young man stared at him, between puffs **of** smoke.

"It occurs to me, Weldon, that you're becoming insolent. It won't do, my boy. Unless you guard your tongue—"

"Bah! Resent it, if you dare; you coward."

"Coward?"

"Yes. A man who attacks an innocent girl is a coward. And you've been a coward all your life, Mershone, for one reason or another. No one believes in your pretended reform. But I want to warn you to keep away from Miss Merrick, hereafter, or I'll take a hand in your punishment myself."

For a moment the two eyed one another savagely. They were equally matched in physique; but Arthur was right, there was no fight in Mershone; that is, of the knock-down order. He would fight in his own way, doubtless, and this made him more dangerous than his antagonist supposed.

"What right have you, sir, to speak for Miss Merrick?" he demanded.

"The best right in the world," replied Arthur. "She is my promised wife."

"Indeed! Since when?"

"That is none of your affair, Mershone. As a matter of fact, however, that little excitement you created last night resulted in a perfect understanding between us."

"*I* created!"

"You, of course. Miss Merrick does not care to meet you again. You will do well to avoid her in the future."

"I don't believe you, Weldon. You're bluffing."

"Am I? Then dare to annoy Miss Merrick again and I'll soon convince you of my sincerity."

With this parting shot he walked away, leaving Mershone really at a loss to know whether he was in earnest or not. To solve the question he called a taxicab and in a few minutes gave his card to the Merrick butler with a request to see Miss Louise.

The man returned with a message that Miss Merrick was engaged.

"Please tell her it is important," insisted Mershone.

Again the butler departed, and soon returned.

"Any message for Miss Merrick must be conveyed in writing, sir," he said. "She declines to see you."

Mershone went away white with anger. We

may credit him with loving Louise as intensely as a man of his caliber can love anyone. His sudden dismissal astounded him and made him frantic with disappointment. Louise's treatment of the past few days might have warned him, but he had no intuition of the immediate catastrophe that had overtaken him. It was n't his self-pride that was injured; that had become so battered there was little of it left; but he had set his whole heart on winning this girl and felt that he could not give her up.

Anger toward Weldon was prominent amongst his emotion. He declared between his set teeth that if Louise was lost to him she should never marry Weldon. Not on Diana's account, but for his own vengeful satisfaction was this resolve made.

He rode straight to his cousin and told her the news. The statement that Arthur was engaged to marry Louise Merrick drove her to a wild anger no less powerful because she restrained any appearance of it. Surveying her cousin steadily through her veiled lashes she asked:

"Is there no way we can prevent this thing?"

Mershone stalked up and down before her like a caged beast. His eyes were red and wicked; his lips were pressed tightly together.

"Diana," said he, "I've never wanted anything in this world as I want that girl. I can't let that mollycoddle marry her!"

She flushed, and then frowned. It was not pleasant to hear the man of her choice spoken of with such contempt, but after all their disappointment and desires were alike mutual and she could not break with Charlie at this juncture.

Suddenly he paused and asked:

"Do you still own that country home near East Orange?"

"Yes; but we never occupy it now. Father does not care for the place."

"Is it deserted?"

"Practically so. Madame Cerise is there in charge."

"Old Cerise? I was going to ask you what had become of that clever female."

"She was too clever, Charlie. She knew too much of our affairs, and was always prying into things that did not concern her. So father took an antipathy to the poor creature, and because she has served our family for so long sent her to care for the house at East Orange."

"Pensioned her, eh? Well, this is good news, Di; perhaps the best news in the world. I believe it will help clear up the situation. Old Cerise and I always understood each other."

"Will you explain?" asked Diana, coldly.

"I think not, my fair cousin. I prefer to keep my own counsel. You made a bad mess of that little deal last night, and are responsible for the climax that faces us. Besides, a woman is never a good conspirator. I know what you want; and I know what I want. So I'll work this plan alone, if you please. And I'll win, Di; I'll win as sure as fate—if you'll help me."

"You ask me to help you and remain in the dark?"

"Yes; it's better so. Write me a note to Cerise and tell her to place the house and herself unreservedly at my disposal."

She stared at him fixedly, and he returned the look with an evil smile. So they sat in silence a moment. Then slowly she arose and moved to her escritoire, drawing a sheet of paper toward her and beginning to write.

"Is there a telephone at the place?" enquired Mershone abruptly.

"Yes."

"Then telephone Cerise after I'm gone. That will make it doubly sure. And give me the number, too, so I can jot it down. I may need it."

Diana quietly tore up the note.

"The telephone is better," she said. "Being in the dark, sir, I prefer not to commit myself in writing."

"You're quite right, Di," he exclaimed, admiringly. "But for heaven's sake don't forget to telephone Madame Cerise."

"I won't Charlie. And, see here, keep your precious plans to yourself, now and always. I intend to know nothing of what you do."

"I'm merely the cats-paw, eh? Well, never mind. Is old Cerise to be depended upon, do you think?"

"Why not?" replied the girl. "Cerise belongs to the Von Taers—body and soul!"

CHAPTER XI

THE BROWN LIMOUSINE

The second evening of the society Kermess passed without unusual event and proved very successful in attracting throngs of fashionable people to participate in its pleasures.

Louise and her cousins were at their stations early, and the second installment of Uncle John's flowers was even more splendid and profuse than the first. It was not at all difficult to make sales, and the little money drawer began to bulge with its generous receipts.

Many a gracious smile or nod or word was bestowed upon Miss Merrick by the society folk; for these people had had time to consider the accusation against her implied by Diana Von Taer's manner when the pearls were discovered in the empty flower vase. Being rather impartial judges—for Diana was not a popular favorite

with her set—they decided it was absurd to suppose a niece of wealthy old John Merrick would
descend to stealing any one's jewelry. Miss Merrick might have anything her heart desired without pausing to count the cost, and moreover she
was credited with sufficient common sense to realize that the Von Taer heirlooms might easily be
recognized anywhere. So a little gossip concerning the queer incident had turned the tide of opin-
ion in Louise's favor, and as she was a recent
debutante with a charming personality all vied
to assure her she was held blameless.

A vast coterie of the select hovered about the
flower booth all the evening, and the cousins joyously realized they had scored one of the distinct
successes of the Kermess. Arthur could not get
very close to Louise this evening; but he enjoyed
her popularity and from his modest retirement was
able to exchange glances with her at intervals,
and these glances assured him he was seldom
absent from her thoughts.

Aside from this, he had the pleasure of glow-
ering ferociously upon Charlie Mershone, who,
failing to obtain recognition from Miss Merrick,

devoted himself to his cousin Diana, or at least lounged nonchalantly in the neighborhood of the Hindoo Booth. Mershone was very quiet. There was a speculative look upon his features that denoted an undercurrent of thought.

Diana's face was as expressionless as ever. She well knew her action of the previous evening had severed the cordial relations formerly existing between her and Mr. Merrick's nieces, and determined to avoid the possibility of a snub by keeping aloof from them. She greeted whoever approached her station in her usual gracious and cultured manner, and refrained from even glancing toward Louise.

Hedrik Von Taer appeared for an hour this evening. He quietly expressed his satisfaction at the complete arrangements of the Kermess, chatted a moment with his daughter, and then innocently marched over to the flower booth and made a liberal purchase from each of the three girls. Evidently the old gentleman had no inkling of the incident of the previous evening, or that Diana was not still on good terms with the young ladies she had personally introduced to society.

His action amused many who noted it, and Louise blushing but thoroughly self-possessed, exchanged her greetings with Diana's father and thanked him heartily for his purchase. Mr. Von Taer stared stonily at Charlie Mershone, but did not speak to him.

Going out he met John Merrick, and the two men engaged in conversation most cordially.

"You did the trick all right, Von Taer," said the little millionaire, "and I'm much obliged, as you may suppose. You're not ashamed of my three nieces, I take it?"

"Your nieces, Mr. Merrick, are very charming young women," was the dignified reply. "They will grace any station in life to which they may be called."

When the evening's entertainment came to an end Arthur Weldon took Louise home in his new brown limousine, leaving Patsy and her father, Uncle John and Beth to comfortably fill the Doyle motor-car. Now that the engagement of the young people had been announced and accepted by their friends, it seemed very natural for them to prefer their own society.

"What do you think of it, Uncle John, any-how?" asked Patsy, as they rode home.

"It's all right, dear," he announced, with a sigh. "I hate to see my girls take the matrimonial dive, but I guess they've got to come to it, sooner or later."

"Later, for me," laughed Patsy.

"As for young Weldon," continued Mr. Mer-rick, reflectively, "he has some mighty good points, as I found out long ago. Also he has some points that need filing down. But I guess he'll average up with most young men, and Louise seems to like him. So let's try to encourage 'em to be happy; eh, my dears?"

"Louise," said Beth, slowly, "is no more per-fect than Arthur. They both have faults which time may eradicate, and as at present they are not disposed to be hypercritical they ought to get along nicely together."

"If 't was me," said the Major, oracularly, "I'd never marry Weldon."

"He won't propose to you, Daddy dear," re-turned Patsy, mischievously; "he prefers Louise."

"I decided long ago," said Uncle John, "that

I'd never be allowed to pick out the husbands for my three girls. Husbands are a matter of taste, I guess, and a girl ought to know what sort she wants. If she don't, and makes a mistake, that's *her* look-out. So you can all choose for yourselves, when the time comes, and I'll stand by you, my dears, through thick and thin. If the husband won't play fair, you can always bet your Uncle John will."

"Oh, we know that," said Patsy, simply; and Beth added: "Of course, Uncle, dear."

Thursday evening, the third and last of the series, was after all the banner night of the great Kermess. All the world of society was present and such wares as remained unsold in the booths were quickly auctioned off by several fashionable gentlemen with a talent for such brigandage. Then, the national dances and songs having been given and received enthusiastically, a grand ball wound up the occasion in the merriest possible way.

Charlie Mershone was much in evidence this evening, as he had been before; but he took no active part in the proceedings and refrained from dancing, his pet amusement. Diana observed that he made frequent trips downstairs, perhaps to the hotel offices. No one paid any attention to his movements, except his cousin, and Miss Von Taer, watching him intently, decided that underneath his calm exterior lurked a great deal of suppressed excitement.

At last the crowd began to disperse. Uncle John and the Major took Beth and Patsy away early, as soon as their booth was closed; but Louise stayed for a final waltz or two with Arthur. She soon found, however, that the evening's work and excitement had tired her, and asked to be taken home.

I'll go and get the limousine around," said Arthur. "That new chauffeur is a stupid fellow. By the time you've managed in this jam to get your wraps I shall be ready. Come down in the elevator and I'll meet you at the Thirty-second street entrance."

As he reached the street a man—an ordinary servant, to judge from his appearance—ran into him full tilt, and when they recoiled from the impact the fellow with a muttered curse raised

his fist and struck young Weldon a powerful blow
Reeling backward, a natural anger seized Arthur,
who was inclined to be hot-headed, and he also
struck out with his fists, never pausing to consider
that the more dignified act would be to call the
police.

The little spurt of fistcuffs was brief, but it gave
Mershone, who stood in the shadow of the doorway near by, time to whisper to a police officer,
who promptly seized the disputants and held them
both in a firm grip.

"What's all this?" he demanded, sternly.

"That drunken loafer assaulted me without
cause'" gasped Arthur, panting.

"It's a lie!" retorted the man, calmly; "he struck
me first."

"Well, I arrest you both," said the officer.

"Arrest!'' cried Arthur, indignantly; "why,
confound it, man, I'm—"

"No talk!" was the stern command. "Come
along and keep quiet."

As if the whole affair had been premeditated
and prearranged a patrol wagon at that instant
backed to the curb and in spite of Arthur Wel-

don's loud protests he was thrust inside with his
assailant and at once driven away at a rapid
gait.

At the same moment a brown limousine drew
up quietly before the entrance.

Louise, appearing in the doorway in ner opera
cloak, stood hesitating on the steps, peering into
the street for Arthur. A man in livery approached
her.

"This way, please, Miss Merrick," he said.
"Mr. Weldon begs you to be seated in the limousine. He will join you in a moment."

With this he led the way to the car and held
the door open, while the girl, having no suspicion,
entered and sank back wearily upon the seat.
Then the door abruptly slammed, and the man in
livery leaped to the seat beside the chauffeur and
with a jerk the car darted away.

So sudden and astounding was this *denouement*
that Louise did not even scream. Indeed, for the
moment her wits were dazed.

And now Charlie Mershone stepped from his
hiding place and with a satirical smile entered the
vestibule and looked at his watch. He found he

had time to show himself again at the Kermess, for a few moments, before driving to the ferry to catch the train for East Orange.

Some one touched him on the arm.

"Very pretty, sir, and quite cleverly done," re- marked a quiet voice.

Mershone started and glared at the speaker, a slender, unassuming man in dark clothes.

"What do you mean, fellow?"

"I've been watching the comedy, sir, and I saw you were the star actor, although you took care to keep hidden in the wings. That bruiser who raised the row took his arrest very easily; I sup- pose you've arranged to pay his fine, and he is n't worried. But the gentleman surely was in hard luck; pounded one minute and pinched the next. You arranged it very cleverly, indeed."

Charlie was relieved that no mention was made of the abduction of Louise. Had that incident escaped notice? He gave the man another sharp look and turned away; but the gentle touch again restrained him.

"Not yet, please, Mr. Mershone."

"Who are you?" asked the other, scowling.

"The house detective. It's my business to watch things. So I noticed you talking to the police officer; I also noticed the patrol wagon standing on the opposite side of the street for nearly an hour—my report on that will amuse them at headquarters, won't it? And I noticed you nod to the bruiser, just as your victim came out."

"Let go of my arm, sir!"

"Do you prefer handcuffs? I arrest you. We'll run over to the station and explain things."

"Do you know who I am?"

"Perfectly, Mr. Mershone. I believe I ran you in for less than this, some two years ago. You gave the name of Ryder, then. Better take another, to-night."

"If you're the house detective, why do you mix up in this affair?" enquired Mershone, his anxiety showing in his tone.

"Your victim was a guest of the house."

"Not at all. He was merely attending the Kermess."

"That makes him our guest, sir. Are you ready?"

Mershone glanced around and then lowered his voice.

"It's all a little joke, my dear fellow," said he, "and you are liable to spoil everything with your bungling. Here," drawing a roll of bills from his pocket, "don't let us waste any more time. I'm busy."

The man chuckled and waved aside the bribe.

"You certainly are, sir; you're *very* busy, just now! But I think the sergeant over at the station will give you some leisure. And listen, Mr. Mershone: I've got it in for that policeman you fixed; he's a cheeky individual and a new man. I'm inclined to think this night's work will cost him his position. And the patrol, which I never can get when I want it, seems under your direct management. These things have got to be explained, and I need your help. Ready, sir?"

Mershone looked grave, but he was not wholly checkmated. Thank heaven the bungling detective had missed the departure of Louise altogether. Charlie's arrest at this critical juncture was most unfortunate, but need not prove disastrous to his cleverly-laid plot. He decided it would be best to go quietly with the "plain-clothes man."

Weldon had become nearly frantic in his demands to be released when Mershone was ushered into the station. He started at seeing his enemy and began to fear a thousand terrible, indefinite things, knowing how unscrupulous Mershone was. But the Waldorf detective, who seemed friendly with the police sergeant, made a clear, brief statement of the facts he had observed. Mershone denied the accusation; the bruiser denied it; the policeman and the driver of the patrol wagon likewise stolidly denied it. Indeed, they had quite another story to tell.

But the sergeant acted on his own judgment. He locked up Mershone, refusing bail. He suspended the policeman and the driver, pending investigation. Then he released Arthur Weldon on his own recognisance, the young man promising to call and testify when required.

The house detective and Arthur started back to the Waldorf together.

"Did you notice a young lady come to the

entrance, soon after I was driven away?" he asked, anxiously.

"A lady in a rose-colored opera cloak, sir?"

"Yes! yes!"

"Why, she got into a brown limousine and rode away."

Arthur gave a sigh of relief.

"Thank goodness that chauffeur had a grain of sense," said he. "I would n't have given him credit for it. Anyway, I'm glad Miss Merrick is safe."

"Huh!" grunted the detective, stopping short. "I begin to see this thing in its true light. How stupid we've been!"

"In what way?" enquired Arthur, uneasily.

"Why did Mershone get you arrested, just at that moment?"

"Because he hated me, I suppose."

"Tell me, could he have any object in spiriting away that young lady—in abducting her?" asked the detective.

"Could he?" cried Arthur, terrified and trembling. "He had every object known to villainy. Come to the hotel! Let's hurry, man—let's fly!"

CHAPTER XII

FOGERTY

At the Waldorf 'Arthur's own limousine was standing by the curb. The street was nearly deserted. The last of the Kermess people had gone home.

Weldon ran to his chauffeur.

"Did you take Miss Merrick home?" he eagerly enquired.

"Miss Merrick? Why, I have n't seen her, sir. I thought you'd all forgotten me."

The young man's heart sank. Despair seized him. The detective was carefully examining the car.

"They're pretty nearly mates, Mr. Weldon, as far as the brown color and general appearances go," he said. "But I'm almost positive the car that carried the young lady away was of another make."

"What make was it?"

The man shook his head.

"Can't say, sir. I was mighty stupid, and that's a fact. But my mind was so full of that assault and battery case, and the trickery of that fellow Mershone, that I was n't looking for anything else."

"Can you get away?" asked Arthur. "Can you help me on this case?"

"No, sir; I must remain on duty at the hotel. But perhaps the young lady is now safe at home, and we've been borrowing trouble. In case she's been stolen, however, you'd better see Fogerty."

"Who's Fogerty?"

"Here's his card, sir. He's a private detective, and may be busy just now, for all I know. But if you can get Fogerty you've got the best man in all New York."

Arthur sprang into the seat beside his driver and hurried post-haste to the Merrick residence. In a few minutes Mrs. Merrick was in violent hysterics at the disappearance of her daughter. Arthur stopped long enough to telephone for a doctor and then drove to the Doyles. He routed up Uncle John and the Major, who appeared in pajamas and bath-robes, and told them the startling news.

A council of war was straightway held. Uncle John trembled with nervousness; Arthur was mentally stupefied; the Major alone was calm.

"In the first place," said he, "what object could the man have in carrying off Louise?"

Arthur hesitated.

"To prevent our marriage, I suppose," he answered. "Mershone has an idea he loves Louise. He made wild love to her until she cut his acquaintance."

"But it won't help him any to separate her from her friends, or her promised husband," declared the Major. "Don't worry. We're sure to find her, sooner or later."

"How? How shall we find her?" cried Uncle John. "Will he murder her, or what?"

"Why, as for that, John, he's safe locked up in jail for the present, and unable to murder anyone," retorted the Major. "It's probable he meant to follow Louise, and induce her by fair means

149

or foul to marry him. But he's harmless enough for the time being."

"It's not for long, though," said Arthur, fearfully. "They're liable to let him out in the morning, for he has powerful friends, scoundrel though he is. And when he is free——"

"Then he must be shadowed, of course," returned the Major, nodding wisely. "If it's true the fellow loves Louise, then he's no intention of hurting her. So make your minds easy. Wherever the poor lass has been taken to, she's probably safe enough."

"But think of her terror—her suffering!" cried Uncle John, wringing his chubby hands. "Poor child! It may be his idea to compromise her, and break her heart!"

"We'll stop all that, John, never fear," promised the Major. "The first thing to do is to find a good detective."

"Fogerty!" exclaimed Arthur, searching for the card.

"Who's Fogerty?"

"I don't know."

"Get the best man possible!" commanded Mr.

Merrick. "Spare no expense; hire a regiment of detectives, if necessary; I'll—"

"Of course you will," interrupted the Major, smiling. "But we won't need a regiment. I'm pretty sure the game is in our hands, from the very start."

"Fogerty is highly recommended," explained Arthur, and related what the house detecive of the Waldorf had said.

"Better go at once and hunt him up," suggested Uncle John. "What time is it?"

"After two o'clock. But I'll go at once."

"Do; and let us hear from you whenever you've anything to tell us," said the Major.

"Where's Patsy?" asked Arthur.

"Sound asleep. Mind ye, not a word of this to Patsy till she *has* to be told. Remember that, John."

"Well, I'll go," said the young man, and hurried away.

Q. Fogerty lived on Eleventh street, according to his card. Arthur drove down town, making good time. The chauffeur asked surlily if this was to be "an all-night job," and Arthur savagely replied that it might take a week. "Can't you see, Jones, that I'm in great trouble?" he added. "But you shall be well paid for your extra time."

"All right, sir. That's no more than just," said the man. "It's none of my affair, you know, if a young lady gets stolen."

Arthur was wise enough to restrain his temper and the temptation to kick Jones out of the limousine. Five minutes later they paused before a block of ancient brick dwellings and found Fogerty's number. A card over the bell bore his name, and Arthur lit a match and read it. Then he rang impatiently.

Only silence.

Arthur rang a second time; waited, and rang again. A panic of fear took possession of him. At this hour of night it would be well-nigh impossible to hunt up another detective if Fogerty failed him. He determined to persist as long as there was hope. Again he rang.

"Look above, sir," called Jones from his station in the car.

Arthur stepped back on the stone landing and looked up. A round spark, as from a cigarette,

was visible at the open window. While he gazed
the spark glowered brighter and illumined a pale,
haggard boy's face, surmounted by tousled locks
of brick colored hair.

"Hi, there!" said Arthur. "Does Mr. Fogerty
live here?"

"He pays the rent," answered a boyish voice,
with a tinge of irony. "What's wanted?"

"Mr. Fogerty is wanted. Is he at home?"

"He is," responded the boy.

"I must see him at once—on important business.
Wake him up, my lad; will you?"

"Wait a minute," said the youth, and left the
window. Presently he opened the front door,
slipped gently out and closed the door behind him.

"Let's sit in your car," he said, in soft, quiet
tones. "We can talk more freely there."

"But I must see Fogerty at once!" protested
Arthur.

"I'm Fogerty."

"Q. Fogerty?"

"Quintus Fogerty—the first and last and only
individual of that name."

Arthur hesitated; he was terribly disappointed.

"Are you a detective?" he enquired.

"By profession."

"But you can't be very old."

The boy laughed.

"I'm no antiquity, sir," said he, "but I've shed the knickerbockers long ago. Who sent you to me?"

"Why do you ask?"

"I'm tired. I've been busy twenty-three weeks. Just finished my case yesterday and need a rest— a good long rest. But if you want a man I'll refer you to a friend."

"Gorman, of the Waldorf, sent me to you— and said you'd help me."

"Oh; that's different. Case urgent, sir?"

"Very. The young lady I'm engaged to marry was abducted less than three hours ago."

Fogerty lighted another cigarette and the match showed Arthur that the young face was deeply lined, while two cold gray eyes stared blankly into his own.

"Let's sit in your limousine, sir," he repeated.

When they had taken their places behind ᵗʰe

closed doors the boy asked Arthur to tell him "all about it, and don't forget any details, please." So Weldon hastily told the events of the evening and gave a history of Mershone and his relations with Miss Merrick. The story was not half told when Fogerty said:

"Tell your man to drive to the police station."

On the way Arthur resumed his rapid recital and strove to post the young detective as well as he was able. Fogerty made no remarks, nor did he ask a single question until Weldon had told him everything he could think of. Then he made a few pointed enquiries and presently they had arrived at the station.

The desk sergeant bowed with great respect to the youthful detective. By the dim light Arthur was now able to examine Fogerty for the first time.

He was small, slim and lean. His face attested to but eighteen or nineteen years, in spite of its deep lines and serious expression. Although his hair was tangled and unkempt Fogerty's clothing and linen were neat and of good quality. He wore a Scotch cap and a horseshoe pin in his cravat.

One might have imagined him to be an errand boy, a clerk, a chauffeur, a salesman or a house man. You might have placed him in almost any middle-class walk in life. Perhaps, thought Arthur, he might even be a good detective! yet his personality scarcely indicated it.

"Mershone in, Billy?" the detective asked the desk sergeant.

"Room 24. Want him?"

"Not now. When is he likely to go?"

"When Parker relieves me. There's been a reg'lar mob here to get Mershone off. I could n't prevent his using the telephone; but I'm a stubborn duck; eh, Quintus? And now the gentleman has gone to bed, vowing vengeance."

"You're all right, Billy. We both know Mershone. Gentleman scoundrel."

"Exactly. Swell society blackleg."

"What name's he docked under?"

"Smith."

"Will Parker let him off with a fine?"

"Yes, or without it. Parker comes on at six."

"Good. I'll take a nap on that bench. Got to keep the fellow in sight, Billy."

"Go into my room. There's a cot there."

"Thanks, old man; I will. I'm dead tired."

Then Fogerty took Arthur aside.

"Go home and try to sleep," he advised. "Don't worry. The young lady's safe enough till Mershone goes to her hiding place. When he does, I'll be there, too, and I'll try to have you with me."

"Do you think you can arrange it alone, Mr. Fogerty?" asked Arthur, doubtfully. The boy seemed so very young.

"Better than if I had a hundred to assist me. Why, this is an easy job, Mr. Weldon. It 'll give me a fine chance to rest up."

"And you won't lose Mershone?"

"Never. He's mine."

"This is very important to me, sir," continued Arthur, nervously.

"Yes; and to others. Most of all it's important to Fogerty. Don't worry, sir."

The young man was forced to go away with this assurance. He returned home, but not to sleep. He wondered vaguely if he had been wise to lean upon so frail a reed as Fogerty seemed to be; and above all he wondered where poor Louise was, and if terror and alarm were breaking her heart.

CHAPTER XIII

DIANA REVOLTS

Charlie Mershone had no difficulty in securing his release when Parker came on duty at six o'clock. He called up a cab and went at once to his rooms at the Bruxtelle; and Fogerty followed him.

While he discarded his dress-coat, took a bath and donned his walking suit Mershone was in a brown study. Hours ago Louise had been safely landed at the East Orange house and placed in the care of old Madame Cerise, who would guard her like an ogre. There was no immediate need of his hastening after her, and his arrest and the discovery of half his plot had seriously disturbed him. This young man was no novice in intrigue, nor even in crime. Arguing from his own standpoint he realized that the friends of Louise were by this time using every endeavor to locate her.

They would not succeed in this, he was positive. His plot had been so audacious and all clews so cleverly destroyed or covered up that the most skillful detective, knowing he had abducted the girl, would be completely baffled in an attempt to find her.

The thought of detectives, in this connection, led him to decide that he was likely to be shadowed. That was the most natural thing for his opponents to do. They could not prove Mershone's complicity in the disappearance of Louise Merrick, but they might easily suspect him, after that little affair of Weldon's arrest. Therefore if he went to the girl now he was likely to lead others to her. Better be cautious and wait until he had thrown the sleuths off his track.

Having considered this matter thoroughly, Mershone decided to remain quiet. By eight o'clock he was breakfasting in the grill room, and Fogerty occupied a table just behind him.

During the meal it occurred to Charlie to telephone to Madame Cerise for assurance that Louise had arrived safely and without a scene to attract the attention of strangers. Having finished breakfast he walked into the telephone booth and was about to call his number when a thought struck him. He glanced out of the glass door. In the hotel lobby were many loungers. He saw a dozen pairs of eyes fixed upon him idly or curiously; one pair might belong to the suspected detective. If he used the telephone there would be a way of discovering the number he had asked for. That would not do—not at all! He concluded not to telephone, at present, and left the booth.

His next act was to purchase a morning paper, and seating himself carelessly in a chair he controlled the impulse to search for a "scare head" on the abduction of Miss Merrick. If he came across the item, very well; he would satisfy no critical eye that might be scanning him by hunting for it with a show of eagerness. The game was in his hands, he believed, and he intended to keep it there.

Fogerty was annoyed by the man's evident caution. It would not be easy to surprise Mershone in any self-incriminating action. But, after all, reflected the boy, resting comfortably in the soft-padded cushions of a big leather chair, all this really made the case the more interesting. He was rather glad Mershone was in no hurry to precipitate a climax. A long stern chase was never a bad chase.

By and bye another idea occurred to Charlie. He would call upon his cousin Diana, and get her to telephone Madame Cerise for information about Louise. It would do no harm to enlighten Diana as to what he had done. She must suspect it already; and was she not a co-conspirator?

But he could not wisely make this call until the afternoon. So meantime he took a stroll into Broadway and walked leisurely up and down that thoroughfare, pausing occasionally to make a trifling purchase and turning abruptly again and again in the attempt to discover who might be following him. No one liable to be a detective of any sort could he discern; yet he was too shrewd to be lulled into a false belief that his each and every act was unobserved.

Mershone returned to his hotel, went to his room, and slept until after one o'clock, as he had secured but little rest the night before in his primitive quarters at the police station. It was

nearly two when he reappeared in the hotel res-
taurant for luncheon, and he took his seat and
ate with excellent appetite.

During this meal Mr. Fogerty also took occasion to refresh himself, eating modestly at a retired table in a corner. Mershone's sharp eyes
noted him. He remembered seeing this youth at
breakfast, and thoughtfully reflected that the boy's
appearance was not such as might be expected
from the guest of a fashionable and high-priced
hotel. Silently he marked this individual as the
possible detective. He had two or three others
in his mind, by this time; the boy was merely
added to the list of possibilities.

Mershone was a capital actor. After luncheon
he sauntered about the hotel, stared from the
window for a time, looked at his watch once or
twice with an undecided air, and finally stepped
to the porter and asked him to call a cab. He
started for Central Park; then changed his mind
and ordered the man to drive him to the Von Taer
residence, where on arrival Diana at once ordered
him shown into her private parlor.

The young man found his cousin stalking up

and down in an extremely nervous manner. She wrung her delicate fingers with a swift, spasmodic motion. Her eyes, nearly closed, shot red rays through their slits.

"What's wrong, Di?" demanded Mershone, considerably surprised by this intense display of emotion on the part of his usually self-suppressed and collected cousin.

"Wrong!" she echoed; "everything is wrong. You've ruined yourself, Charlie; and you're going to draw me into this dreadful crime, also, in spite of all I can do!"

"Bah! don't be a fool," he observed, calmly taking a chair.

"Am *I* the fool?" she exclaimed, turning upon him fiercely. "Did *I* calmly perpetrate a deed that was sure to result in disgrace and defeat?"

"What on earth has happened to upset you?" he asked, wonderingly. "It strikes me everything is progressing beautifully."

"Does it, indeed?" was her sarcastic rejoinder. "Then your information is better than mine. They called me up at three o'clock this morning to enquire after Louise Merrick—as if *I* should know her whereabouts. Why did they come to *me* for such information? Why?" she stamped her foot for emphasis.

"I suppose," said Charlie Mershone, "they called up everyone who knows the girl. It would be natural in case of her disappearance."

"Come here!" cried Diana, seizing his arm and dragging him to a window. "Be careful; try to look out without showing yourself. Do you see that man on the corner?"

"Well?"

"He has been patrolling this house since daybreak. He's a detective!"

Charlie whistled.

"What makes you think so, Di? Why on earth should they suspect you?"

"Why? Because my disreputable cousin planned the abduction, without consulting me, and—"

"Oh, come, Di; that's a little too—"

"Because the girl has been carried to the Von Taer house—*my* house—in East Orange; because my own servant is at this moment her jailor, and—"

"How should they know all this?" interrupted Mershone, impatiently. "And how do you happen to know it yourself, Diana?"

"Madame Cerise called me up at five o'clock, just after Louise's uncle had been here for the second time, with a crew of officers. Cerise is in an ugly mood. She said a young girl had been brought to her a prisoner, and Mr. Mershone's orders were to keep her safely until he came. She is greatly provoked at our using her in this way, but promised to follow instructions if I accepted all responsibility."

"What did you tell her?"

"That I knew nothing of the affair, but had put the house and her services at your disposal. I said I would accept no responsibility whatever for anything you might do."

Mershone looked grave, and scowled.

"The old hag won't betray us, will she?" he asked, uneasily.

"She cannot betray me, for I have done nothing. Charlie," she said, suddenly facing him, "I won't be mixed in this horrid affair. You must carry out your infamous plan in your own way.

I know nothing, sir, of what you have done; I know nothing of what you intend to do. Do you understand me?"

He smiled rather grimly.

"I hardly expected, my fair cousin, that you would be frightened into retreat at this stage of the game, when the cards are all in our hands. Do you suppose I decided to carry away Louise without fully considering what I was doing, and the immediate consequences of my act? And wherein have I failed? All has gone beautifully up to this minute. Diana, your fears are absolutely foolish, and against your personal interests. All that I am doing for myself benefits you doubly. Just consider, if you will, what has been accomplished for our mutual benefit: The girl has disappeared under suspicious circumstances; before she again rejoins her family and friends she will either be my wife or Arthur Weldon will prefer not to marry her. That leaves him open to appreciate the charms of Diana Von Taer, does it not? Already, my dear cousin, your wishes are accomplished. My own task, I admit, is a harder one, because it is more delicate."

The cold-blooded brutality of this argument caused even Diana to shudder. She looked at the young man half fearfully as she asked:

"What is your task?"

"Why, first to quiet Louise's fears; then to turn her by specious arguments—lies, if you will —against Weldon; next to induce her to give me her hand in honest wedlock. I shall tell her of my love, which is sincere; I shall argue—threaten, if necessary; use every reasonable means to gain her consent."

"You'll never succeed!" cried Diana, with conviction.

"Then I'll try other tactics," said he blandly.

"If you do, you monster, I'll expose you," warned the girl.

"Having dissolved partnership, you won't be taken into my confidence, my fair cousin. You have promised to know nothing of my acts, and I'll see you don't." Then he sprang from his chair and came to her with a hard, determined look upon his face. "Look here, Di; I've gone too far in this game to back out now. I'm going to carry it through if it costs me my life and liberty—and yours into the bargain! I love Louise Merrick! I love her so well that without her the world and its mockeries can go to the devil! There's nothing worth living for but Louise—Louise. She's going to be my wife, Diana—by fair means or foul I swear to make her my wife."

He had worked himself up to a pitch of excitement surpassing that of Diana. Now he passed his hand over his forehead, collected himself with a slight shudder, and resumed his seat.

Diana was astonished. His fierce mood served to subdue her own. Regarding him curiously for a time she finally asked:

"You speak as if you were to be allowed to have your own way—as if all society was not arrayed against you. Have you counted the cost of your action? Have you considered the consequences of this crime?"

"I have committed no crime," he said stubbornly. "All's fair in love and war."

"The courts will refuse to consider that argument, I imagine," she retorted. "Moreover, the friends of this kidnaped girl are powerful and active. They will show you no mercy if you are discovered."

"If I fail," answered Mershone, slowly, "I do not care a continental what they do to me, for my life will be a blank without Louise. But I really see no reason to despair, despite your womanish croakings. All seems to be going nicely and just as I had anticipated."

"I am glad that you are satisfied," Diana returned, with scornful emphasis. "But understand me, sir; this is none of my affair in any way—except that I shall surely expose you if a hair of the girl's head is injured. You must not come here again. I shall refuse to see you. You ought not to have come to-day."

"Is there anything suspicious in my calling upon my cousin—as usual?"

"Under such circumstances, yes. You have not been received at this house of late years, and my father still despises you. There is another danger you have brought upon me. My father seemed suspicious this morning, and asked me quite pointedly what I knew of this strange affair."

"But of course you lied to him. All right,

Diana; perhaps there is nothing to be gained
from your alliance, and I'll let you out of the deal
from this moment. The battle's mine, after all,
and I'll fight it alone. But—I need more money.
You ought to be wiling to pay, for so far the
developments are all in your favor."

She brought a handful of notes from her desk.

"This ends our partnership, Charlie," she said.

"Very well. A women makes a poor conspirator, but is invaluable as a banker."

"There will be no more money. This ends
everything between us."

"I thought you were game, Di. But you're as
weak as the ordinary feminine creation."

She did not answer, but stood motionless, a
defiant expression upon her face. He laughed a
little, bowed mockingly, and went away.

CHAPTER XIV

A COOL ENCOUNTER

On leaving the house Mershone buttoned his overcoat tightly up to his chin, for the weather was cold and raw, and then shot a quick glance around him. Diana's suspect was still lounging on the corner. Charlie had little doubt he was watching the house and the movements of its inmates—a bad sign, he reflected, with a frown. Otherwise the street seemed deserted.

He had dismissed the cab on his arrival, so now he stepped out and walked briskly around the corner, swinging his cane jauntily and looking very unlike a fugitive. In the next block he passed a youth who stood earnestly examining the conventional display in a druggist's window.

Mershone, observing this individual, gave a start, but did not alter his pace. It was the same pale, red-haired boy he had noticed twice before at the hotel. In his alert, calculating mind there was no coincidence in this meeting. Before he had taken six more steps Mershone realized the exact situation.

At the next crossing he stopped and waited patiently for a car. Up the street he still saw the youth profoundly interested in drugs—a class of merchandise that seldom calls for such close inspection. The car arrived and carried Mershone away. It also left the red-haired youth at his post before the window. Yet on arriving at the Bruxtelle some twenty minutes later Charlie found this same queer personage occupying a hotel chair in the lobby and apparently reading a newspaper with serious attention.

He hesitated a moment, then quietly walked over to a vacant chair beside the red-haired one and sat down. The youth turned the paper, glanced casually at his neighbor, and continued reading.

"A detective, I believe," said Mershone, in a low, matter of fact tone.

"Who? me?" asked Fogerty, lowering the paper.

"Yes. Your age deceived me for a time. I imagined you were a newsboy or a sporting kid from the country; but now I observe you are older than you appear. All sorts of people seem to drift into the detective business. I suppose your present occupation is shadowing me."

Fogerty smiled. The smile was genuine.

"I might even be a lawyer, sir," he replied, "and in that case I should undertake to cross-examine you, and ask your reasons for so queer a charge."

"Or you might be a transient guest at this hotel," the other returned, in the same bantering tone, "for I saw you at breakfast and luncheon: Pretty fair *chef* here, is n't he? But you did n't stick to that part, you know. You followed me up-town, where I made a call on a relative, and you studied the colored globes in a druggist's window when I went away. I wonder why people employ inexperienced boys in such important matters. In your case, my lad, it was easy enough to detect the detective. You even took the foolish chance of heading me off, and returned to this hotel before I did. Now, then, is my charge unfounded?"

"Why should you be under the surveillance of a detective?" asked Fogerty, slowly.

"Really, my boy, I cannot say. There was an unpleasant little affair last night at the Waldorf, in which I was not personally concerned, but suffered, nevertheless. An officious deputy caused my arrest and I spent an unpleasant night in jail. There being nothing in the way of evidence against me I was released this morning, and now I find a detective shadowing me. What can it all mean, I wonder? These stupid blunders are very annoying to the plain citizen, who, however innocent, feels himself the victim of a conspiracy."

"I understand you, sir," said Fogerty, drily.

For some moments Mershone now remained silent. Then he asked: "What are your instructions concerning me?"

To his surprise the boy made a simple, frank admission.

"I'm to see you don't get into more mischief, sir."

"And how long is this nonsense to continue?"

demanded Mershone, showing a touch of anger for the first time.

"Depends on yourself, Mr. Mershone; I'm no judge, myself. I'm so young—and inexperienced."

"Who is your employer?"

"Oh, I'm just sent out by an agency."

"Is it a big paying proposition?" asked Charlie, eyeing the diffident youth beside him critically, as if to judge his true caliber.

"Not very big. You see, if I'd been a better detective you'd never have spotted me so quickly."

"I suppose money counts with you, though, as it does with everyone else in the world?"

"Of course, sir. Every business is undertaken to make money."

Mershone drew his chair a little nearer.

"I need a clever detective myself," he announced, confidentially. "I'm anxious to discover what enemy is persecuting me in this way. Would it—er—be impossible for me to employ *you* to—er—look after my interests?"

Fogerty was very serious.

"You see, sir," he responded, "if I quit this job

they may not give me another. In order to be a successful detective one must keep in the good graces of the agencies."

"That's easy enough," asserted Mershone. "You may pretend to keep this job, but go home and take life easy. I'll send you a daily statement of what I've been doing, and you can fix up a report to your superior from that. In addition to this you can put in a few hours each day trying to find out who is annoying me in this rascally manner, and for this service I'll pay you five times the agency price. How does that proposition strike you, Mr.——"

"Riordan. Me name's Riordan," said Fogerty, with a smile. "No, Mr. Mershone," shaking his head gravely, "I can't see my way to favor you. It's an easy job now, and I'm afraid to take chances with a harder one."

Something in the tone nettled Mershone.

"But the pay," he suggested.

"Oh, the pay. If I'm a detective fifty years, I'll make an easy two thousand a year. That's a round hundred thousand. Can you pay me that much to risk my future career as a detective?"

Mershone bit his lip. This fellow was not so simple, after all, boyish as he seemed. And, worse than all, he had a suspicion the youngster was baiting him, and secretly laughing at his offers of bribery.

"They will take you off the job, now that I have discovered your identity," he asserted, with malicious satisfaction.

"Oh, no," answered Fogerty; "they won't do that. This little interview merely simplifies matters. You see, sir, I'm an expert at disguises. That's my one great talent, as many will testify. But you will notice that in undertaking this job I resorted to no disguise at all. You see me as nature made me—and 't was a poor job, I'm thinking."

"Why were you so careless?"

"It was n't carelessness; it was premeditated. There's not the slightest objection to your knowing me. My only business is to keep you in sight, and I can do that exactly as well as Riordan as I could by disguising myself."

Mershone had it on his tongue's end to ask what they expected to discover by shadowing him, but decided it was as well not to open an avenue for the discussion of Miss Merrick's disappearance. So, finding he could not bribe the youthful detective or use him in any way to his advantage, he closed the interview by rising.

"I'm going to my room to write some letters," said he, with a yawn. "Would you like to read them before they are mailed?"

Again Fogerty laughed in his cheerful, boyish way.

"You'd make a fine detective yourself, Mr. Mershone," he declared, "and I advise you to consider the occupation. I've a notion it's safer, and better pay, than your present line."

Charlie scowled at the insinuation, but walked away without reply. Fogerty eyed his retreating figure a moment, gave a slight shrug and resumed his newspaper.

Day followed day without further event, and gradually Mershone came to feel himself trapped. Wherever he might go he found Fogerty on duty, unobtrusive, silent and watchful. It was very evident that he was waiting for the young man to lead him to the secret hiding place of Louise Merrick.

In one way this constant surveillance was a distinct comfort to Charlie Mershone, for it assured him that the retreat of Louise was still undiscovered. But he must find some way to get rid of his "shadow," in order that he might proceed to carry out his plans concerning the girl. During his enforced leisure he invented a dozen apparently clever schemes, only to abandon them again as unpractical.

One afternoon, while on a stroll, he chanced to meet the bruiser who had attacked Arthur Weldon at the Waldorf, and been liberally paid by Mershone for his excellent work. He stopped the man, and glancing hastily around found that Fogerty was a block in the rear.

"Listen," he said; "I want your assistance, and if you're quick and sure there is a pot of money waiting for you."

"I need it, Mr. Mershone," replied the man, grinning.

"There's a detective following me; he's down

the street there—a mere boy—just in front of that tobacco store. See him?"

"Sure I see him. It's Fogerty."

"His name is Riordan."

"No; it's Fogerty. He's no boy, sir, but the slickest 'tec' in the city, an' that's goin' some, I can tell you."

"Well, you must get him, whoever he is. Drag him away and hold him for three hours—two—one. Give me a chance to slip him; that's all. Can you do it? I'll pay you a hundred for the job."

"It's worth two hundred, Mr. Mershone. It is n't safe to fool with Fogerty."

"I'll make it two hundred."

"Then rest easy," said the man. "I know the guy, and how to handle him. You just watch him like he's watching you, Mr. Mershone, and if anything happens you skip as lively as a flea. I can use that two hundred in my business."

Then the fellow passed on, and Fogerty was still so far distant up the street that neither of them could see the amused smile upon his thin face.

CHAPTER XV

A BEWILDERING EXPERIENCE

When Louise Merrick entered the brown limousine, which she naturally supposed to belong to Arthur Weldon, she had not the faintest suspicion of any evil in her mind. Indeed, the girl was very happy this especial evening, although tired with her duties at the Kermess. A climax in her young life had arrived, and she greeted it joyously, believing she loved Arthur well enough to become his wife.

Now that the engagement had been announced to their immediate circle of friends she felt as proud and elated as any young girl has a right to be under the circumstances.

Added to this pleasant event was the social triumph she and her cousins had enjoyed at the Kermess, where Louise especially had met with rare favor. The fashionable world had united in being most kind and considerate to the dainty, attractive young *debutante,* and only Diana had seemed to slight her. This was not surprising in view of the fact that Diana evidently wanted Arthur for herself, and there was some satisfaction in winning a lover who was elsewhere in prime demand. In addition to all this the little dance that concluded the evening's entertainment had been quite delightful, and all things conspired to put Louise in a very contented frame of mind.

Still fluttering with the innocent excitements of the hour the girl went to join Arthur without a fear of impending misfortune. She did not think of Charlie Mershone at all. He had been annoying and impertinent, and she had rebuked him and sent him away, cutting him out of her life altogether. Perhaps she ought to have remembered that she had mildly flirted with Diana's cousin and given him opportunity for the impassioned speeches she resented; but Louise had a girlish idea that there was no harm in flirting, considering it a feminine license. She saw young Mershone at the Kermess that evening paying indifferent attentions to other women and ignoring her, and was sincerely glad to have done with him for good and all.

She obeyed readily the man who asked her to be seated in the limousine. Arthur would be with her in a minute, he said. When the door closed and the car started she had an impulse to cry out, but next moment controlled it and imagined they were to pick up Mr. Weldon on some corner.

On and on they rolled, and still no evidence of the owner of the limousine. What could it mean, Louise began to wonder. Had something happened to Arthur, so that he had been forced to send her home alone? As the disquieting thought came she tried to speak with the chauffeur, but could not find the tube. The car was whirling along rapidly; the night seemed very dark, only a few lights twinkled here and there ouside.

Suddenly the speed slackened. There was a momentary pause, and then the machine slowly rolled upon a wooden platform. A bell clanged, there was a whistle and the sound of revolving water-wheels. Louise decided they must be upon a ferry-boat, and became alarmed for the first time.

The man in livery now opened the door, as if to reassure her.

"Where are we? Where is Mr. Weldon?" enquired the girl, almost hysterically.

"He is on the boat, miss, and will be with you shortly now," replied the man, very respectfully. "Mr. Weldon is very sorry to have annoyed you, Miss Merrick, but says he will soon explain everything, so that you will understand why he left you."

With this he quietly closed the door again, although Louise was eager to ask a dozen more questions. Prominent was the query why they should be on a ferry-boat instead of going directly home. She knew the hour must be late.

But while these questions were revolving in her mind she still suspected no plot against her liberty. She must perforce wait for Arthur to explain his queer conduct; so she sat quietly enough in her place awaiting his coming, while the ferry puffed steadily across the river to the Jersey shore.

The stopping of the boat aroused Louise from her reflections. Arthur not here yet? Voices were calling outside; vehicles were noisily leaving their positions on the boat to clatter across the platforms. But there was no sign of Arthur.

Again Louise tried to find the speaking tube. Then she made an endeavor to open the door, although just then the car started with a jerk that flung her back against the cushions.

The knowledge that she had been grossly deceived by her conductor at last had the effect of arousing the girl to a sense of her danger. Something must be wrong. Something *was* decidedly wrong, and fear crept into her heart. She pounded on the glass windows with all her strength, and shouted as loudly as she could, but all to no avail.

Swiftly the limousine whirled over the dusky road and either her voice could not be heard through the glass cage in which she was confined or there was no one near who was willing to hear or to rescue her.

She now realized how wrong she had been to sit idly during the trip across the ferry, where a score of passengers would gladly have assisted her. How cunning her captors had been to lull her fears during that critical period! Now, alas, it was too late to cry out, and she had no idea where she was being taken or the reason of her going.

Presently it occurred to her that this was not Arthur's limousine at all. There was no speaking tube for one thing. She leaned forward and felt for the leathern pocket in which she kept a veil and her street gloves. No pocket of any sort was to be found.

An unreasoning terror now possessed her. She knew not what to fear, yet feared everything. She made another attempt to cry aloud for help and then fell back unconscious on the cushions.

How long she lay in the faint she did not know. When she recovered the limousine was still rattling forward at a brisk gait but bumping over ruts in a manner that indicated a country road.

Through the curtains she could see little but the black night, although there was a glow ahead cast by the searchlights of the car. Louise was weak and unnerved. She had no energy to find a way to combat her fate, if such a way were possible. A dim thought of smashing a window and hurling herself through it gave her only a shudder of repulsion. She lacked strength for such a desperate attempt.

On, on, on. Would the dreary journey never end? How long must she sit and suffer before she could know her fate, or at least find some explanation of the dreadful mystery of this wild midnight ride?

At last, when she had settled down to dull despair, the car came to a paved road and began to move more slowly. It even stopped once or twice, as if the driver was not sure of his way. But they kept moving, nevertheless, and before long entered a driveway. There was another stop now, and a long wait.

Louise lay dismally back upon the cushions, sobbing hysterically into her dripping handkerchief. The door of her prison at last opened and a light shone in upon her.

"Here we are, miss," said the man in uniform, still in quiet, respectful tones. "Shall I assist you to alight?"

She started up eagerly, her courage returning

with a bound. Stepping unassisted to the ground she looked around her in bewilderment.

The car stood before the entrance to a modest country house. There was a light in the hall and another upon the broad porch. Around the house a mass of trees and shrubbery loomed dark and forbidding.

"Where am I?" demanded Louise, drawing back haughtily as the man extended a hand toward her.

"At your destination, miss," was the answer. "Will you please enter?"

"No! Not until I have an explanation of this— this—singular, high-handed proceeding," she replied, firmly.

Then she glanced at the house. The hall door had opened and a woman stood peering anxiously at the scene outside.

With sudden resolve Louise sprang up the steps and approached her. Any woman, she felt, in this emergency, was a welcome refuge.

"Who are you?" she asked eagerly, "and why have I been brought here?"

"*Mademoiselle* will come inside, please," said

the woman, with a foreign accent. "It is cold in the night air, *N'est-ce-pas?*

She turned to lead the way inside. While Louise hesitated to follow the limousine started with a roar from its cylinders and disappeared down the driveway, the two men going with it. The absence of the lamps rendered the darkness around the solitary house rather uncanny. An intense stillness prevailed except for the diminishing rattle of the receding motor car. In the hall was a light and a woman.

Louise went in.

CHAPTER XVI

MADAME CERISE, CUSTODIAN

The woman closed the hall door and locked it. Then she led the way to a long, dim drawing-room in which a grate fire was smouldering. A stand lamp of antique pattern but dimly illuminated the place, which seemed well furnished in an old fashioned way.

"Will not you remove your wraps, Mees— Mees—I do not know ma'm'selle's name."

"What is your own name?" asked Louise, coming closer to gaze earnestly into the other's face.

"I am called Madame Cerise, if it please you."

Her voice, while softened to an extent by the French accent, was nevertheless harsh and emotionless. She spoke as an automaton, slowly, and pausing to choose her words. The woman was of medium size, slim and straight in spite of many years. Her skin resembled brown parchment; her eyes were small, black and beady; her nose somewhat fleshy and her lips red and full as those of a young girl. The age of Madame Cerise might be anywhere between fifty and seventy; assuredly she had long been a stranger to ·youth, although her dark hair was but slightly streaked with gray. She wore a somber-hued gown and a maid's jaunty apron and cap.

Louise inspected her closely, longing to find a friend and protector in this curious and strange woman. Her eyes were moist and pleading—an appeal hard to resist. But Madame Cerise returned her scrutiny with a wholly impassive expression.

"You are a French maid?" asked Louise, softly.

"A housekeeper, ma'm'selle. For a time, a caretaker."

"Ah, I understand. Are your employers asleep?"

"I cannot say, ma'm'selle. They are not here."

"You are alone in this house?"

"Alone with you, ma'm'selle."

Louise had a sudden access of alarm.

"And why am I here?" she cried, wringing her hands pitifully.

"Ah, who can tell that?" returned the woman, composedly. "Not Cerise, indeed. Cerise is told nothing—except what is required of her. I but obey my orders."

Louise turned quickly, at this.

"What are your orders, then?" she asked.

"To attend ma'm'selle with my best skill, to give her every comfort and care, to—"

"Yes—yes!"

"To keep her safely until she is called for. That is all."

The girl drew a long breath.

"Who will call for me, then?"

"I am not inform, ma'm'selle."

"And I am a prisoner in this house?"

"Ma'm'selle may call it so, if it please her. But reflect; there is no place else to go. It is bleak weather, the winter soon comes. And here I can make you the comforts you need."

Louise pondered this speech, which did not deceive her. While still perplexed as to her abduction, with no comprehension why she should have been seized in such a summary manner and spirited to this lonely, out-of-the-way place, she realized she was in no immediate danger. Her weariness returned tenfold, and she staggered and caught the back of a chair for support.

The old woman observed this.

"Ma'm'selle is tired," said she. "See; it is past four by the clock, and you must be much fatigue by the ride and the nervous strain."

"I—I'm completely exhausted," murmured Louise, drooping her head wearily. The next moment she ran and placed her hands on Madame Cerise's shoulders, peering into the round, beady eyes with tender pleading as she continued: "I don't know why I have been stolen away from my home and friends; I don't know why this dreadful thing has happened to me; I only know that I am worn out and need rest. Will you take care of me, Madame Cerise? Will you watch over me while I sleep and guard me from all harm? I—I have n't any mother to lean on now, you know; I have n't any friend at all— but *you!*"

The grim features never relaxed a muscle; but a softer look came into the dark eyes and the woman's voice took on a faint tinge of compassion as she answered:

"Nothing can harm ma'm'selle. Have no fear, *ma chere*. I will take care of you; I will watch. *Allons!* it is my duty; it is also my pleasure."

"Are there no—no men in the house—none at all?" enquired the girl, peering into the surrounding gloom nervously.

"There is no person at all in the house, but you and I."

"And you will admit no one?"

The woman hesitated.

"Not to your apartment," she said firmly. "I promise it."

Louise gave a long, fluttering sigh. Somehow, she felt that she could rely upon this promise.

"Then, if you please, Madame Cerise, I'd like to go to bed," she said.

The woman took the lamp and led the way upstairs, entering a large, airy chamber in which a fire burned brightly in the grate. The furniture here was dainty and feminine. In an alcove stood a snowy bed, the covers invitingly turned down.

Madame Cerise set the lamp upon a table and

without a word turned to assist Louise. The beautiful Kermess costume, elaborately embroidered with roses, which the girl still wore, evidently won the Frenchwoman's approval. She unhooked and removed it carefully and hung it in a closet. Very dextrous were her motions as she took down the girl's pretty hair and braided it for the night. A dainty *robe de nuit* was provided.

"It is my own," she said simply. "Ma'm'selle is not prepared."

"But there must be young ladies in your family," remarked Louise, thoughtfully, for in spite of the stupor she felt from want of sleep the novelty of her position kept her alert in a way. It is true she was too tired and bewildered to think clearly, but slight details were impressing themselves upon her dimly. "This room, for instance—"

"Of course, *ma chere*, a young lady has lived here. She has left some odd pieces of wardrobe behind her, at times, in going away. When you waken we will try to find a house-dress to replace your evening gown. Will ma'm'selle indulge in the bath before retiring?"

"Not to-night, Madame Cerise. I'm too tired for anything but—sleep!"

Indeed, she had no sooner crawled into the enticing bed than she sank into unconscious forgetfulness. This was to an extent fortunate. Louise possessed one of those dispositions cheery and equable under ordinary circumstances, but easily crushed into apathy by any sudden adversity. She would not suffer so much as a more excitable and nervous girl might do under similar circumstances.

Her sleep, following the severe strain of the night's adventure, did little to refresh her. She awoke in broad daylight to hear a cold wind whistling shrilly outside and raindrops beating against the panes.

Madame Cerise had not slept much during the night. For an hour after Louise retired she sat in her room in deep thought. Then she went to the telephone and notwithstanding the late hour called up Diana, who had a branch telepone on a table at her bedside.

Miss Von Taer was not asleep. She had had an exciting night herself. She answered the old caretaker readily and it did not surprise her to learn that the missing girl had been taken to the East Orange house by the orders of Charlie Mershone. She enquired how Louise had accepted the situation forced upon her, and was shocked and rendered uncomfortable by the too plainly worded protest of the old Frenchwoman. Madame Cerise did not hesitate to denounce the abduction as a heartless crime, and in her communication with Diana swore she would protect the innocent girl from harm at the hands of Mershone or anyone else.

"I have ever to your family been loyal and true, Ma'm'selle Diana," said she, "but I will not become the instrument of an abominable crime at your command or that of your wicked cousin. I will keep the girl here in safety, if it is your wish; but she will be safe, indeed, as long as Cerise guards her."

"That's right, Madame," stammered Diana, hardly knowing at the moment what to say. "Be discreet and silent until you hear from me again;

guard the girl carefully and see that she is not too unhappy; but for heaven's sake keep Charlie's secret until he sees fit to restore Miss Merrick to her friends. No crime is contemplated; I would not allow such a thing, as you know. Yet it is none of my affair whatever. My cousin has compromised me by taking the girl to my house, and no knowledge of the abduction must get abroad if we can help it. Do you understand me?"

"No," was the reply. "The safest way for us all is to send Miss Merrick away."

"That will be done as soon as possible."

With this the old Frenchwoman was forced to be content, and she did not suspect that her report had made Miss Von Taer nearly frantic with fear—not for Louise but for her own precious reputation. Accustomed to obey the family she had served for so many years, Madame Cerise hesitated to follow her natural impulse to set the poor young lady free and assist her to return to her friends. So she compromised with her conscience—a thing she was not credited with possessing—by resolving to make the imprisonment of the *"pauvre fille"* as happy as possible.

Scarcely had Louise opened her eyes the following morning when the old woman entered her chamber, unlocking the door from the outside to secure admission.

She first rebuilt the fire, and when it was crackling cheerfully she prepared a bath and brought an armful of clothing which she laid out for inspection over the back of a sofa. She produced lingerie, too, and Louise lay cuddled up in the bedclothes and watched her keeper thoughtfully until the atmosphere of the room was sufficiently warmed.

"I'll get up, now," she said, quietly.

Madame Cerise was assuredly a skilled lady's maid. She bathed the girl, wrapped her in an ample kimono and then seated her before the dresser and arranged her *coiffure* with dextrous skill.

During this time Louise talked. She had decided her only chance of escape lay in conciliating this stern-faced woman, and she began by relating her entire history, including her love affair with Arthur Weldon, Diana Von Taer's attempt to rob her of her lover, and the part that Charlie Mershone had taken in the affair.

Madame Cerise listened, but said nothing.

"And now," continued the girl, "tell me who you think could be so wicked and cruel as to carry me away from my home and friends? I cannot decide myself. You have more experience and more shrewdness, can't you tell me, Madame Cerise?"

The woman muttered inaudibly.

"Mr. Mershone might be an enemy, because I laughed at his love-making," continued Louise, musingly. "Would a man who loved a girl try to injure her? But perhaps his love has turned to hate. Anyhow, I can think of no one else who would do such a thing, or of any reason why Charlie Mershone should do it."

Madame Cerise merely grunted. She was brushing the soft hair with gentle care.

"What could a man gain by stealing a girl? If it was Mr. Mershone, does he imagine I could ever forget Arthur? Or cease to love him? Or that Arthur would forget me while I am away? Perhaps it's Diana, and she wants to get rid of me so she can coax Arthur back to her side. But that's nonsense; is n't it, Madame Cerise? No girl—not even Diana Von Taer—would dare to act in such a high-handed manner toward her rival. Did you ever hear of Miss Von Taer? She's quite a society belle. Have you ever seen her, Madame Cerise?"

The woman vouchsafed no reply to this direct enquiry, but busied herself dressing the girl's hair. Louise casually turned over the silver-mounted hand mirror she was holding and gave a sudden start. A monogram was engraved upon the metal: "D. v. T." She gazed at the mark fixedly and then picked up a brush that the Frenchwoman laid down. Yes, the same monogram appeared upon the brush.

The sharp eyes of Cerise had noted these movements. She was a little dismayed but not startled when Louise said, slowly: " 'D. v. T.' stands for Diana Von Taer. And it is n't likely to stand for anything else. I think the mystery is explained, now, and my worst fears are realized. Tell me, Madame, is this Diana Von Taer's house?"

Her eyes shone with anger and round red patches suddenly appeared upon her pallid cheeks. Madame Cerise drew a long breath.

"It used to be," was her quiet answer. "It was left her by her grandmother; but Mr. Von Taer did not like the place and they have not been here lately—not for years. Miss Von Taer informed me, some time ago, that she had transferred the property to another."

"To her cousin—Mr. Mershone?" asked Louise quickly.

"That may be the name; I cannot remember," was the evasive reply.

"But you must know him, as he is Diana's cousin," retorted Louise. "Why will you try to deceive me? Am I not helpless enough already, and do you wish to make me still more miserable?"

"I have seen Mr. Mershone when he was a boy, many times. He was not the favorite with Ma'm-'selle Diana, nor with Monsieur Von Taer. For myself, I hated him."

There was decided emphasis to the last sentence. Louise believed her and felt a little relieved.

From the *mélange* of apparel a modest outfit was obtained to clothe the girl with decency and comfort, if not in the prevailing style. The fit left much to be desired, yet Louise did not complain, as weightier matters were now occupying her mind.

The toilet completed, Madame Cerise disappeared to get a tray containing a good breakfast. She seemed exceedingly attentive.

"If you will give me the proper directions I will start for home at once," announced Louise, with firm resolve, while eating her egg and toast.

"I am unable to give you directions, and I cannot let you go, ma'm'selle," was the equally firm reply. "The day is much too disagreeable to venture out in, unless one has proper conveyance. Here, alas, no conveyance may be had."

Louise tried other tactics.

"I have no money, but several valuable jewels," she said, meaningly. "I am quite sure they will obtain for me a conveyance."

"You are wrong, ma'm'selle; there is no conveyance to be had!" persisted the old woman, more sternly.

"Then I shall walk."

"It is impossible."

"Where is this place situated? How far is it from New York? How near am I to a street-car, or to a train?"

"I cannot tell you."

"But this is absurd!" cried Louise. "You cannot deceive me for long. I know this is Diana Von Taer's house, and I shall hold Diana Von Taer responsible for this enforced imprisonment."

"That," said Madame Cerise, coldly, "is a matter of indifference to me. But ma'm'selle must understand one thing, she must not leave this house."

"Oh, indeed!"

"At least, until the weather moderates," added the woman, more mildly.

She picked up the tray, went to the door and passed out. Louise heard the key click in the lock.

CHAPTER XVII

THE MYSTERY DEEPENS

Uncle John was both astounded and indignant that so bold and unlawful an act as the abduction of his own niece could have been perpetrated in the heart of New York and directly under the eyes of the police. Urged by the Major, Mr. Merrick was at first inclined to allow Arthur Weldon to prosecute the affair and undertake the recovery of the girl, being assured this would easily be accomplished and conceding the fact that no one had a stronger interest in solving the mystery of Louise's disappearance than young Weldon. But when midday arrived and no trace of the young girl had yet been obtained the little millionaire assumed an important and decisive air and hurried down town to "take a hand in the game" himself.

After a long interview with the Chief of Detectives, Mr. Merrick said impressively:

"Now, understand, sir; not a hint of this to the newspaper folks. I won't have any scandal attached to the poor child if I can help it. Set your whole force to work—at once!—but impress them with the need of secrecy. My offer is fair and square. I'll give a reward of ten thousand dollars if Miss Merrick is discovered within twenty-four hours; nine thousand if she's found during the next twenty-four hours; and so on, deducting a thousand for each day of delay. That's for the officer who finds her. For yourself, sir, I intend to express my gratitude as liberally as the service will allow me to. Is this all clear and above-board?"

"It is perfectly clear, Mr. Merrick."

"The child must be found—and found blamed quick, too! Great Cæsar! Can a simple affair like this baffle your splendid metropolitan force?"

"Not for long, Mr. Merrick, believe me."

But this assurance proved optimistic. Day by day crept by without a clew to the missing girl being discovered; without development of any

sort. The Inspector informed Mr. Merrick that
"it began to look like a mystery."

Arthur, even after several sleepless nights, still
retained his courage.

"I'm on the right track, sir," he told Uncle
John. "The delay is annoying, but not at all dangerous. So long as Fogerty holds fast to Mershone Louise is safe, wherever she may be."

"Mershone may have nothing to do with the
case."

"I'm positive he has."

"And Louise can't be safe while she's a prisoner,
and in the hands of strangers. I want the girl
home! Then I'll know she's safe."

"I want her home, too, sir. But all your men
are unable to find her, it seems. They can't even
discover in what direction she was taken, or how.
The brown limousine seems to be no clue at all."

"Of course not. There are a thousand brown
limousines in New York."

"Do you imagine she's still somewhere in the
city, sir?" enquired Arthur.

"That's my theory," replied Uncle John. "She
must be somewhere in the city. You see it would

be almost impossible to get her out of town without discovery. But I'll admit this detective force is the finest aggregation of incompetents I've ever known—and I don't believe your precious Fogerty is any better, either."

Of course Beth and Patsy had to be told of their cousin's disappearance as soon as the first endeavor to trace her proved a failure. Patsy went at once to Mrs. Merrick and devoted herself to comforting the poor woman as well as she could.

Beth frowned at the news and then sat down to carefully think out the problem. In an hour she had logically concluded that Diana Von Taer was the proper person to appeal to. If anyone knew where Louise was, it was Diana. That same afternoon she drove to the Von Taer residence and demanded an interview.

Diana was at that moment in a highly nervous state. She had at times during her career been calculating and unscrupulous, but never before had she deserved the accusation of being malicious and wicked. She had come to reproach herself bitterly for having weakly connived at the desperate act of Charlie Mershone, and her good sense assured her the result would be disastrous to all concerned in it. Contempt for herself and contempt for her cousin mingled with well-defined fears for her cherished reputation, and so it was that Miss Von Taer had almost decided to telephone Madame Cerise and order her to escort Louise Merrick to her own home when Beth's card came up with a curt demand for a personal interview.

The natures of these two girls had never harmonized in the slightest degree. Beth's presence nerved Diana to a spirit of antagonism that quickly destroyed her repentant mood. As she confronted her visitor her demeanor was cold and suspicious. There was a challenge and an accusation in Beth's eyes that conveyed a distinct warning, which Miss Von Taer quickly noted and angrily resented—perhaps because she knew it was deserved.

It would have been easy to tell Beth De Graf where her cousin Louise was, and at the same time to assure her that Diana was blameless in the affair; but she could not endure to give her antagonist this satisfaction.

Beth began the interview by saying: "What have you done with Louise Merrick?" That was, of course, equal to a declaration of war.

Diana was sneering and scornful. Thoroughly on guard, she permitted no compromising word or admission to escape her. Really, she knew nothing of Louise Merrick, having unfortunately neglected to examine her antecedents and personal characteristics before undertaking her acquaintance. One is so likely to blunder through excess of good nature. She had supposed a niece of Mr. John Merrick would be of the right sort; but the age is peculiar, and one cannot be too cautious in choosing associates. If Miss Merrick had run away from her home and friends, Miss Von Taer was in no way responsible for the escapade. And now, if Miss De Graf had nothing further to say, more important matters demanded Diana's time.

Beth was furious with anger at this baiting. Without abandoning a jot her suspicions she realized she was powerless to prove her case at this time. With a few bitter and cutting remarks—made, she afterward said, in "self-defense"—she retreated as gracefully as possible and drove home.

An hour later she suggested to Uncle John that he have a detective placed where Diana's movements could be watched; but that had already been attended to by both Mr. Merrick and Mr. Fogerty. Uncle John could hardly credit Diana's complicity in this affair. The young lady's social position was so high, her family so eminently respectable, her motive in harming Louise so inconceivable, that he hesitated to believe her guilty, even indirectly. As for her cousin, he did not know what to think, as Arthur accused him unreservedly. It did not seem possible that any man of birth, breeding and social position could be so contemptible as to perpetrate an act of this character. Yet some one had done it, and who had a greater incentive than Charlie Mershone?

Poor Mrs. Merrick was inconsolable as the days dragged by. She clung to Patsy with pitiful entreaties not to be left alone; so Miss Doyle brought her to her own apartments, where the bereft woman was shown every consideration. Vain and selfish though Mrs. Merrick might be, she was passionately devoted to her only child, and her fears for the life and safety of Louise were naturally greatly exaggerated.

The group of anxious relatives and friends canvassed the subject morning, noon and night, and the longer the mystery remained unsolved the more uneasy they all became.

"This, ma'am," said Uncle John, sternly, as he sat one evening facing Mrs. Merrick, "is the final result of your foolish ambition to get our girls into society."

"I can't see it that way, John," wailed the poor woman. "I've never heard of such a thing happening in society before, have you?"

"I don't keep posted," he growled. "But everything was moving smoothly with us before this confounded social stunt began, as you must admit."

"I can't understand why the papers are not full of it," sighed Mrs. Merrick, musingly. "Louise is so prominent now in the best circles."

"Of course," said the Major, drily; "she's so prominent, ma'am, that no one can discover her at all! And it's lucky for us the newspapers know nothing of the calamity. They'd twist the thing into so many shapes that not one of us would ever again dare to look a friend in the eye."

"I'm sure my darling has been murdered!" declared Mrs. Merrick, weeping miserably. She made the statement on an average of once to every five minutes. "Or, if she has n't been killed yet, she's sure to be soon. Can't *something* be done?"

That last appeal was hard to answer. They had done everything that could be thought of. And here it was Tuesday. Louise had been missing for five days.

CHAPTER XVIII

A RIFT IN THE CLOUDS

The Tuesday morning just referred to dawned cold and wintry. A chill wind blew and for a time carried isolated snowflakes whirling here and there. Gradually, as the morning advanced, the flakes became more numerous, until by nine o'clock an old fashioned snowstorm had set in that threatened to last for some time. The frozen ground was soon covered with a thin white mantle and the landscape in city and country seemed especially forbidding.

In spite of these adverse conditions Charlie Mershone decided to go out for a walk. He felt much like a prisoner, and his only recreation was in getting out of the hotel for a daily stroll. Moreover, he had an object in going abroad to-day.

So he buttoned his overcoat up to his chin and fearlessly braved the storm. He had come to wholly disregard the presence of the detective who shadowed him, and if the youthful Fogerty by chance addressed him he was rewarded with a direct snub. This did not seem to disconcert the boy in the least, and to-day, as usual, when Mershone walked out Fogerty followed at a respectful distance. He never appeared to be watching his man closely, yet never for an instant did Mershone feel that he had shaken the fellow off.

On this especial morning the detective was nearly a block in the rear, with the snow driving furiously into his face, when an automobile suddenly rolled up to the curb beside him and two men leaped out and pinioned Fogerty in their arms. There was no struggle, because there was no resistance. The captors quickly tossed the detective into the car, an open one, which again started and turned into a side street.

Fogerty, seated securely between the two burly fellows, managed to straighten up and rearrange his clothing.

"Will you kindly explain this unlawful act, gentlemen?" he enquired.

The man on the left laughed aloud. He was

the same individual who had attacked Arthur
Weldon, the one who had encountered Mershone
in the street the day before.

"Cold day, ain't it, Fogerty?" he remarked.
"But that makes it all the better for a little auto
ride. We like you, kid, we're fond of you—awful
fond—ain't we, Pete?"

"We surely are," admitted the other.

"So we thought we'd invite you out for a whirl
—see? We'll give you a nice ride, so you can enjoy the scenery. It's fine out Harlem way, an' the
cold'll make you feel good. Eh, Pete?"

"That's the idea," responded Pete, cheerfully.

"Very kind of you," said the detective, leaning
back comfortably against the cushions and pulling
up his coat collar to shield him from the wind.
"But are you aware that I'm on duty, and that this
will allow my man to slip away from me?"

"Can't help that; but we're awful sorry," was
the reply. "We just wanted company, an' you're
a good fellow, Fogerty, considerin' your age an'
size."

"Thank you," said Fogerty. "You know me,
and I know you. You are Bill Leesome, alias Will

Dutton—usually called Big Bill. You did time a couple of years ago for knocking out a policeman."

"I'm safe enough now, though," responded Big Bill. "You're not working on the reg'lar force, Fogerty, you're only a private burr."

"I am protected, just the same," asserted Fogerty. "When you knabbed me I was shadowing Mershone, who has made away with a prominent society young lady."

"Oh, he has, has he?" chuckled Big Bill, and his companion laughed so gleefully that he attracted Fogerty's attention to himself.

"Ah, I suppose you are one of the two men who lugged the girl off," he remarked; "and I must congratulate you on having made a good job of it. Is n't it curious, by the way, that the fellow who stole and hid this girl should be the innocent means of revealing her hiding place?"

The two men stared at him blankly. The car, during this conversation, had moved steadily on, turning this and that corner in a way that might have confused anyone not perfectly acquainted with this section of the city.

"What d'ye mean by that talk, Fogerty?" demanded Big Bill.

"Of course it was Mershone who stole the girl," explained the detective, calmly; "we know that. But Mershone is a clever chap. He knew he was watched, and so he has never made a movement to go to his prisoner. But he grew restless in time, and when he met you, yesterday, fixed up a deal with you to carry me away, so he could escape."

Big Bill looked uncomfortable.

"You know a lot, Fogerty," he said, doggedly.

"Yes; I've found that human nature is much the same the world over," replied the detective. "Of course I suspected you would undertake to give Mershone 'his chance by grabbing me, and that is exactly what you have done. But, my lads, what do you suppose I have done in the meantime?"

They both looked their curiosity but said nothing.

"I've simply used your clever plot to my own advantage, in order to bring things to a climax," continued Fogerty. "While we are joy-riding here, a half dozen of my men are watching every move that Mershone makes. I believe he will lead them straight to the girl; don't you?

Big Bill growled some words that were not very choice and then yelled to the chauffeur to stop. The other man was pale and evidently frightened.

"See here, Fogerty; you make tracks!" was the sharp command, as the automobile came to a halt. "You've worked a pretty trick on us, 'cordin' to your own showin', and we must find Mr. Mershone before it's too late—if we can."

"Good morning," said Fogerty, alighting. "Thank you for a pleasant ride—and other things."

They dashed away and left him standing on the curb; and after watching them disappear the detective walked over to a drug store and entered the telephone booth.

"That you, Hyde?—This is Fogerty."

"Yes, sir. Mr. Mershone has just crossed the ferry to Jersey. Adams is with him. I'll hear from him again in a minute; hold the wire."

Fogerty waited. Soon he learned that Mershone had purchased a ticket for East Orange. The train would leave in fifteen minutes.

Fogerty decided quickly. After looking at his watch he rushed out and arrested a passing taxicab.

"Ready for a quick run—perhaps a long one?" he asked.

"Ready for anything," declared the man.

The detective jumped in and gave hurried directions.

"Never mind the speed limit," he said. "No one will interfere with us. I'm Fogerty."

CHAPTER XIX

POLITIC REPENTANCE

Perhaps no one—not even Mrs. Merrick—was so unhappy in consequence of the lamentable crime that had been committed as Diana Von Taer. Immediately after her interview with Beth her mood changed, and she would have given worlds to be free from complicity in the abduction. Bitterly, indeed, she reproached herself for her enmity toward the unsuspecting girl, an innocent victim of Diana's own vain desires and Charles Mershone's heartless wiles. Repenting her folly and reasoning out the thing when it was too late, Diana saw clearly that she had gained no possible advantage, but had thoughtlessly conspired to ruin the reputation of an honest, ingenuous girl.

Not long ago she had said that her life was dull, a stupid round of social functions that bored her dreadfully. She had hoped by adopting John

Merrick's nieces as her *protégées* and introducing them to society to find a novel and pleasurable excitement that would serve to take her out of her unfortunate *ennui*—a condition to which she had practically been born.

But Diana had never bargained for such excitement as this; she had never thought to win self abhorrence by acts of petty malice and callous cruelties.

Yet so intrenched was she in the conservatism of her class that she could not at once bring herself to the point of exposing her own guilt that she might make amends for what had been done. She told herself she would rather die than permit Louise to suffer through her connivance with her reckless, unprincipled cousin. She realized perfectly that she ought to fly, without a moment's delay, to the poor girl's assistance. Yet fear of exposure, of ridicule, of loss of caste, held her a helpless prisoner in her own home, where she paced the floor and moaned and wrung her hands until she was on the verge of nervous prostration. If at any time she seemed to acquire sufficient courage to go to Louise, a glance at the detective watching the house unnerved her and prevented her from carrying out her good intentions.

You must not believe that Diana was really bad; her lifelong training along set lines and practical seclusion from the everyday world were largely responsible for her evil impulses. Mischief is sure to crop up, in one form or another, among the idle and ambitionless. More daring wickedness is said to be accomplished by the wealthy and aimless creatures of our false society than by the poorer and uneducated classes, wherein criminals are supposed to thrive. These sins are often unpublished, although not always undiscovered, but they are no more venial because they are suppressed by wealth and power.

Diana Von Taer was a girl who, rightly led, might have been capable of developing a noble womanhood; yet the conditions of her limited environment had induced her to countenance a most dastardly and despicable act. It speaks well for the innate goodness of this girl that she at last actually rebelled and resolved to undo, insofar as she was able, the wrong that had been accomplished.

For four days she suffered tortures of remorse. On the morning of the fifth day she firmly decided to act. Regardless of who might be watching, or of any unpleasant consequences to herself, she quietly left the house, unattended, and started directly for the East Orange mansion.

CHAPTER XX

A TELEPHONE CALL

Still another laggard awoke to action on this eventful Tuesday morning.

Madame Cerise had been growing more and more morose and dissatisfied day by day. Her grievance was very tangible. A young girl had been brought forcibly to the house and placed in her care to be treated as a prisoner. From that time the perpetrators of the deed had left the woman to her own resources, never communicating with her in any way.

During a long life of servitude Madame Cerise had acquiesced in many things that her own conscience did not approve of, for she considered herself a mere instrument to be used at will by the people who employed and paid her. But her enforced solitude as caretaker of the lonely house at East Orange had given her ample time to think,

226

and her views had lately undergone a decided change.

To become the jailer of a young, pretty and innocent girl was the most severe trial her faithfulness to her employers had ever compelled her to undergo, and the woman deeply resented the doubtful position in which she had been placed.

However, the chances were that Madame Cerise might have obeyed her orders to the letter had not so long a period of waiting ensued. During these days she was constantly thrown in the society of Louise, which had a tendency to make her still more rebellious. The girl clung to Cerise in her helplessness and despair, and constantly implored her to set her free. This, indeed, the Frenchwoman might have done long ago had she not suspected such an act might cause great embarrassment to Diana Von Taer, whom she had held on her knee as an infant and sought to protect with loyal affection.

It was hard, though, to hear the pitiful appeals of the imprisoned girl, and to realize how great was the wrong that was being done her. The old woman was forced to set her jaws firmly and turn

deaf ears to the pleadings in order not to succumb
to them straightway. Meantime she did her duty
conscientiously. She never left Louise's room
without turning the key in the lock, and she stead-
fastly refused the girl permission to wander in
the other rooms of the house. The prison was a
real prison, indeed, but the turnkey sought to al-
leviate the prisoner's misery by every means in her
power. She was indefatigable in her service,
keeping the room warm and neat, attending to the
girl's every want and cooking her delicious meals.

While this all tended to Louise's comfort it
had little affect in soothing her misery. Between
periods of weeping she sought to cajole the old
woman to release her, and at times she succumbed
to blank despair. Arthur was always in her mind,
and she wondered why he did not come to rescue
her. Every night she stole softly from her bed
to try the door, hoping Cerise had forgotten to
lock it. She examined her prison by stealth to discover any possible way of escape.

There were two small windows and one large
one. The latter opened upon the roof of a small
porch, but there was no way to descend from it

unless one used a frail lattice at one end, which in summer probably supported a rose or other vine. Louise shrank intuitively from such a desperate undertaking. Unless some dreadful crisis occurred she would never dare trust herself to that frail support. Yet it seemed the only possible way of escape.

Time finally wore out the patience of Madame Cerise, who was unable longer to withstand Louise's pleadings. She did not indicate by word or look that her attitude had changed, but she made a secret resolve to have done with the affair altogether.

Often in their conversations the girl had mentioned Arthur Weldon. She had given Cerise his address and telephone number, and implored her at least to communicate with him and tell him his sweetheart was safe, although unhappy. This had given the old woman the clever idea on which she finally acted.

By telephoning Mr. Weldon she could give him the information that would lead to his coming for Louise, without anyone knowing who it was that had betrayed the secret. This method commended itself strongly to her, as it would save her from any trouble or reproach.

Leaving Louise at breakfast on this Tuesday morning Madame Cerise went down to the telephone and was soon in communication with Arthur. She told him, in a quiet tone, that Miss Louise Merrick was being secluded in a suburban house near East Orange, and described the place so he could easily find it. The young man questioned her eagerly, but aside from the information that the girl was well and uninjured she vouchsafed no further comment.

It was enough, however. Arthur, in wild excitement, rushed to the rescue.

CHAPTER XXI

THE UNEXPECTED HAPPENS

Madame Cerise, well knowing she had accelerated the march of events to a two-step, calmly sat herself down in the little housekeeper's room off the lower hall and, leaving Louise to her moody solitude upstairs, awaited the inevitable developments.

Outside the weather was cold and blustering. The wind whirled its burden of snowflakes in every direction with blinding, bewildering impartiality. It was a bad day to be out, thought the old Frenchwoman; but a snowstorm was not likely to deter an anxious lover. She calculated the time it would take Monsieur Weldon to arrive at the mansion: if he was prompt and energetic he could cover the distance in an hour and a half by train or three hours by motor car. But he must prepare for the journey, and that would consume some time; perhaps she need not expect him within two hours at the earliest.

She read, to pass away the time, selecting a book from a shelf of well-worn French novels. Somehow she did not care to face her tearful prisoner again until she could restore the unhappy girl to the arms of her true lover. There was still romance in the soul of Madame Cerise, however withered her cheeks might be. She was very glad that at last she had summoned courage to act according to the dictates of her heart.

Eh? What is this? A rumble of wheels over the frozen snow caused her to glance at the clock above the mantel. Not by any possibility could Monsieur Weldon arrive so soon. Who, then, could it be?

She sat motionless while the doorbell rang, and rang again. Nothing must interfere with the pretty *denouement* she had so fondly anticipated when Louise's faithful knight came to her.

But the one who had just now alighted was persistent. The vehicle had been sent away—she heard the sound of receding wheels—and the new arrival wanted to get in. The bell jerked and jangled unceasingly for a time and then came a crash against the door, as if a stalwart shoulder was endeavoring to break it down.

Madame Cerise laid down her book, placed her *pince-nez* in the case, and slowly proceeded down the hall. The door shook with another powerful impact, a voice cried out demanding admittance.

"Who is it, then?" she called shrilly.

"Open the door, confound you!" was the irritated reply.

The woman reflected. This was surely young Mershone's voice. And she had no excuse to deny him admittance. Quietly she unbolted the door and allowed it to open an inch while she peered at the man outside.

"Oh! it is Monsieur Mershone."

"Of course it is," he roared, forcing the door open and stalking in. "Who in thunder did you think it was?"

"A thousand pardons, m'sieur," said Cerise. "I must be cautious; it is your own command. That you may be protected I deny admittance to all."

"That's all right," said Mershone gruffly, while he stamped his feet upon the rug and shook the

233

snow from his clothing. "Have n't you any fire in this beastly old refrigerator? I'm nearly frozen. Where's Miss Merrick?"

"She is occupying Ma'm'selle Diana's room, in the west wing. Will monsieur please to come this way?"

She led him to her own little room, and so engrossed were they that neither remembered he had failed to rebolt the front door.

A good fire burned in the grate of Cerise's cosy den and Mershone threw off his overcoat and warmed his hands as he showered questions upon the old caretaker.

"How is the girl behaving? Tears and hysterics?"

"At times, m'sieur."

"Takes it hard, eh?"

"She is very unhappy."

"Ever mention a man named Weldon?"

"Often."

"Humph!" He did not like this report. "Has anyone been here to disturb you, or to make enquiries?"

"No one, m'sieur."

"We're safe enough, I guess. It was a mighty neat job, Cerise, taken altogether, although the fools have been watching me night and day. That's the reason I did not come sooner."

She made no comment. Mershone threw himself into a chair and stared thoughtfully at the fire.

"Has Louise—Miss Merrick, you know—mentioned my name at all?"

"At times."

"In what way?"

"With loathing and contempt."

He scowled at her savagely.

"Do you think she suspects that I carried her away?"

"She seems to know it absolutely."

He stared at the fire again.

"I've got a queer job on my hands, Cerise, and I rely on you to help me," said he presently, assuming a more conciliating manner. "Perhaps I'm in a box, or a hole, or whatever else you like to call it, but it's too late too back down now—I must push ahead and win. You see the case is this: I love the girl and had her brought here to keep her from another man. By hook or crook I'm going to make her my wife. She won't take kindly to that at first, perhaps, but I'll make her happy in the end. In one way this delay has been a good thing. It must have worn her out and broken her spirits quite a bit; eh?"

"She seems very miserable," conceded the woman.

"Do you find her hard to manage? Does she show much temper? In other words, do you suppose she'll put up a fight?"

Madame Cerise regarded him wonderingly.

"She is a good girl," was her reply. "She loves with much devotion the man from whom you have stolen her. I am quite positive she will never consent to become your wife."

"Oh, you are? Well, I intend she shall marry me, and that settles it. She's unnerved and miserable now, and I mean to grind her down till she has n't strength to resist me. That sounds hard, I know; but it's the only way to accomplish my purpose. After she's my wife I'll be very kind to her, poor thing, and teach her to love me. A man can do anything with a woman if he sets about it the right way. I'm not taking this stand because I'm cruel, Cerise, but because I'm desperate. All's fair in love and war, you know, and this is a bit of both."

He was pacing the floor by this time, his hands thrust deep in his pockets, an anxious look upon his face that belied his bombastic words.

The Frenchwoman's expression was impassive. Her scorn for the wretch before her was tempered with the knowledge that his cowardly plan was doomed to defeat. It was she who had checkmated him, and she was glad. Now and again her eyes sought the clock, while she silently calculated the time to elapse before Arthur Weldon arrived. There would be a pretty scene then, Cerise would have much enjoyment in witnessing the encounter.

"Now, then, take me to Louise," commanded Mershone, suddenly.

She shrank back in dismay.

"Oh, not yet, m'sieur!"

"Why not?"

"The young lady is asleep. She will not waken for an hour—perhaps two."

"I can't wait. We'll waken her now, and give her an idea of the change of program."

"But no, m'sieur! It is outrageous. The poor thing has but now sobbed herself to sleep, after many bitter hours. Can you not wait a brief hour, having waited five days?"

"No. Take me to her at once."

As he came toward her the woman drew away.

"I cannot," she said firmly.

"See here, Cerise, I intend to be obeyed. I won't endure any nonsense at this stage of the game, believe me," he announced fiercely. "In order to win, there's just one way to manage this affair, and I insist upon your following my instructions. Take me to Louise!"

"I will not!" she returned, the bead-like eyes glittering as they met his angry gaze.

"Then I'll go alone. Give me the key."

She did not move, nor did she answer him. At her waist hung a small bunch of household keys and this he seized with a sudden movement and jerked loose from its cord.

"You miserable hag!" he muttered, inflamed with anger at her opposition. "If you propose to defend this girl and defy me, you'll find I'm able to crush you as I will her. While I'm gone I expect you to come to your · senses, and decide to obey me."

With these words he advanced to the door of the little room and opened it. Just outside stood Fogerty, smiling genially.

"Glad to meet you again, Mr. Mershone," he said. "May I come in? ' Thank you."

While Mershone stood bewildered by this unexpected apparition the detective entered the room, closed the door carefully, and putting his back to it bowed politely to Madame Cerise.

"Pardon this seeming intrusion, ma'am," said he. "I'm here on a little matter of business, having a warrant for the arrest of Mr. Charles Connoldy Mershone."

CHAPTER XXII

GONE

The grim face of Madame Cerise relaxed to allow a quaint smile to flit across it. She returned Fogerty's bow with a deep curtsy.

Mershone, after one brief exclamation of dismay, wrested from him by surprise, threw himself into the chair again and stared at the fire. For a few moments there was intense stillness in the little room.

"How easy it is," said Fogerty, in soft, musing tones, "to read one's thoughts—under certain circumstances. You are thinking, Mr. Mershone, that I'm a boy, and not very strong, while you are an athlete and can easily overpower me. I have come at a disagreeable time, and all your plans depend on your ability to get rid of me. But I've four good men within call, who are just now guarding the approaches to this house. They'd like to come in, I know, because it's very cold and disagreeable outside; but suppose we allow them to freeze for a time? Ah, I thought you'd agree with me, sir—I overheard you say you were about to visit Miss Merrick, who is confined in a room upstairs, but I'd like you to postpone that while we indulge in a little confidential chat together. You see—"

The door-bell rang violently. Fogerty glanced at Madame Cerise.

"Will you see who it is?" he asked.

She arose at once and left the room. Mershone turned quickly.

"What's your price, Fogerty?" he asked, meaningly.

"For what?"

"For getting out of here—making tracks and leaving me alone. Every man has his price, and I'm trapped—I'm willing to pay anything—I'll—"

"Cut it out, sir. You've tried this once before. I'm not to be bribed."

"Have you really a warrant for my arrest?"

"I've carried it since Friday. It's no use, Mershone, the game's up and you may as well grin and bear it."

Mershone was about to reply when the door opened and Diana Von Taer came in with a swift, catlike tread and confronted him with flaming eyes.

"You coward! You low, miserable scoundrel! How dare you come here to annoy and browbeat that poor girl?" she cried in clear, cutting accents, without noticing the presence of Fogerty.

"Oh, shut up, Di, you're in it as deep as I am," he retorted, turning away with a flushed face.

"I'm not, sir! Never have I countenanced this wicked, criminal act," she declared. "I have come here to-day to save Louise from your wiles and carry her back to her friends. I dare you, or your confederates," with a scornful look at the detective, "to interfere with me in any way." Then she turned to Cerise and continued: "Where is Miss Merrick now?"

"In your own room, ma'm'selle."

"Come with me, then."

With a defiant glance at Mershone she turned haughtily and left the room. Cerise followed obediently, somewhat astonished at the queer turn of events.

Left alone with Mershone, Fogerty chuckled gleefully.

"Why, it seems I was n't needed, after all," said he, "and we've both of us taken a lot of trouble for nothing, Mershone. The chances are Miss Von Taer would have turned the trick in any event, don't you think so?"

"No, you don't understand her. She would n't have interfered if she had n't been scared out," growled the other. "She's sacrificed me to save herself, that's all."

"You may be right about that," admitted Fogerty; and then he got up to answer the door-bell, which once more rang violently.

An automobile stood outside, and from it an excited party trooped into the hallway, disregarding the cutting wind and blinding snowflakes that assailed them as they passed in. There was Arthur Weldon and Uncle John, Patricia and Beth; and all, as they saw the detective, cried with one voice:

"Where's Louise?"

Fogerty had just managed to close the door against the wintry blast when the answer came from the stairway just above:

"She is gone!"

The voice was shrill and despairing, and looking up they saw Diana standing dramatically posed upon the landing, her hands clasped over her heart and a look of fear upon her face. Over her shoulder the startled black eyes of old Cerise peered down upon the group below.

The newcomers were evidently bewildered by this reception. They had come to rescue Louise, whom they imagined confined in a lonely deserted villa with no companion other than the woman who guarded her. Arthur's own detective opened the door to them and Diana Von Taer, whom they certainly did not expect to meet here, confronted them with the thrilling statement that Louise had gone.

Arthur was the first to recover his wits.

"Gone!" he repeated; "gone where?"

"She had escaped—run away!" explained Diana, in real distress.

"When?" asked Uncle John.

"Just now. Wtihin an hour, was n't it, Ce-rise?"

"At ten o'clock I left her, now she is gone," said the old woman, who appeared as greatly agitated as her mistress.

"Good gracious! you don't mean to say she's left the house in this storm?" exclaimed Patsy, aghast at the very thought.

"What shall we do? What *can* we do?" demanded Beth, eagerly.

Fogerty started up the stairs. Cerise turned to show him the way, and the others followed in an awed group.

The key was in the lock of the door to the missing girl's room, but the door itself now stood ajar. Fogerty entered, cast a sharp look around and walked straight to the window. As the others came in, glancing curiously about them and noting the still smouldering fire and the evidences of recent occupation, the detective unlatched the French window and stepped out into the snow that covered the roof of the little porch below. Arthur sprang out beside him, leaving the rest to shiver in the cold blast that rushed in upon them from the open window.

Fogerty, on his knees, scanned the snow carefully, and although Weldon could discover no sign of a footprint the young detective nodded his head sagaciously and slowly made his way to the trellis at the end. Here it was plain that the accumulation of snow had recently been brushed away from the frail framework.

"It was strong enough to hold her, though," declared Fogerty, looking over the edge of the roof. "I'll descend the same way, sir. Go back by the stairs and meet me below."

He grasped the lattice and began cautiously to lower himself to the ground, and Arthur turned to rejoin his friends in the room.

"That is the way she escaped, without doubt," he said to them. "Poor child, she had no idea we were about to rescue her, and her long confinement had made her desperate."

"Did she have a cloak, or any warm clothes?" asked Beth. Madame Cerise hurriedly examined the wardrobe in the closets.

"Yes, ma'm'selle; she has taken a thick coat

and a knit scarf," she answered. But I am sure she had no gloves, and her shoes were very thin."

"How long do you think she has been gone?" Patsy enquired.

"Not more than an hour. I was talking with Mr. Mershone, and—"

"Mershone! Is he here?" demanded Arthur.

"He is in my room downstairs—or was when you came," said the woman.

"That accounts for her sudden flight," declared the young man, bitterly. "She doubtless heard his voice and in a sudden panic decided to fly. Did Mershone see her?" he asked.

"No, m'sieur," replied Cerise.

With one accord they descended to the lower hall and the caretaker led the way to her room. To their surprise they found Mershone still seated in the chair by the fire, his hands clasped behind his head, a cigarette between his lips.

"Here is another crime for you to account for!" cried Arthur, advancing upon him angrily. "You have driven Louise to her death!"

Mershone raised one hand in mild protest.

"Don't waste time cursing me," he said. "Try to find Louise before it is too late."

The reproach seemed justified. Arthur paused and turning to Mr. Merrick said:

"He is right. I'll go help Fogerty, and you must stay here and look after the girls until we return."

As he went out he passed Diana without a look. She sat in a corner of the room sobbing miserably. Beth was thoughtful and quiet, Patsy nervous and indignant. Uncle John was apparently crushed by the disaster that had overtaken them. Mershone's suggestion that Louise might perish in the storm was no idle one; the girl was not only frail and delicate but worn out with her long imprisonment and its anxieties. They all realized this.

"I believe," said Mershone, rising abruptly, "I'll go and join the search. Fogerty has arrested me, but you needn't worry about my trying to escape. I don't care what becomes of me, now, and I'm going straight to join the detective."

They allowed him to go without protest, and he buttoned his coat and set out in the storm to find the others. Fogerty and Arthur were by this time in the lane back of the grounds, where the detective was advancing slowly with his eyes fixed on the ground.

"The tracks are faint, but easily followed," he was saying, "The high heels of her shoes leave a distinct mark."

When Mershone joined them Arthur scowled at the fellow but said nothing. Fogerty merely smiled.

From the lane the tracks, already nearly obliterated by the fast falling snow, wandered along nearly a quarter of a mile to a crossroads, where they became wholly lost.

Fogerty looked up and down the roads and shook his head with a puzzled expression.

"We've surely traced her so far," said he, "but now we must guess at her further direction. You'll notice this track of a wagon. It may have passed fifteen minutes or an hour ago. The hoof tracks of the horses are covered, so I'm not positive which way they headed; I only know there are indications of hoof tracks, which proves it a farmer's wagon. The question is, whether the young lady met it, and caught a ride, or whether she proceeded along some of the other trails. I can't find any indication of those high-heeled shoes from this point, in any direction. Better get your car, Mr. Weldon, and run east a few miles, keeping sharp watch of the wagon tracks on the way. It was a heavy wagon, for the wheels cut deep. Mershone and I will go west. When you've driven far enough to satisfy yourself you're going the wrong direction, you may easily overtake us on your return. Then, if we've discovered nothing on this road, we'll try the other."

Arthur ran back at once to the house and in a few minutes had started on his quest. The motor car was powerful enough to plow through the deep snow with comparative ease.

Those left together in Madam Cerise's little room were more to be pitied than the ones engaged in active search, for there was nothing to relieve their fears and anxieties. Diana, unable to bear the accusing looks of Patsy and Beth, resolved to make a clean breast of her complicity in the affair and related to them every detail of her connection with her cousin's despicable plot. She ended by begging their forgiveness, and wept so miserably that Uncle John found himself stroking her hair while Patsy came close and pressed the penitent girl's hand as if to comfort and reassure her.

Beth said nothing. She could not find it in her heart as yet to forgive Diana's selfish conspiracy against her cousin's happiness. If Louise perished in this dreadful storm the proud Diana Von Taer could not escape the taint of murder. The end was not yet.

CHAPTER XXIII

THE CRISIS

Mershone and Fogerty plodded through the snow together, side by side. They were facing the wind, which cut their faces cruelly, yet neither seemed to mind the bitterness of the weather.

"Keep watch along the roadside," suggested Mershone; "she may have fallen anywhere, you know. She could n't endure this thing long. Poor Louise!"

"You were fond of her, Mr. Mershone?" asked Fogerty, not unsympathetically.

"Yes. That was why I made such a struggle to get her."

"It was a mistake, sir. Provided a woman is won by force or trickery she's never worth getting. If she does n't care for you it's better to give her up."

"I know—now."

"You're a bright fellow, Mershone, a clever fellow. It's a pity you could n't direct your talents the right way. They'll jug you for this."

"Never mind. The game of life is n't worth playing. I've done with it, and the sooner I go to the devil the better. If only I could be sure Louise was safe I'd toss every care—and every honest thought—to the winds, from this moment."

During the silence that followed Fogerty was thoughtful. Indeed, his mind dwelt more upon the defeated and desperate man beside him than upon the waif he was searching for.

"What's been done, Mr. Mershone," he said, after a time, "can't be helped now. The future of every man is always a bigger proposition than his past—whoever he may be. With your talents and genius you could yet make of yourself a successful and prosperous man, respected by the community—if you could get out of this miserable rut that has helped to drag you down."

"But I can't," said the other, despondently.

"You can if you try. But you'll have to strike for a place a good way from New York. Go West, forget your past, and carve out an honest future under a new name and among new. associates. You're equal to it."

Mershone shook his head.

"You forget," he said. "They'll give me a jail sentence for this folly, as sure as fate, and that will be the end of me."

"Not necessarily. See here, Mershone, it won't help any of those people to prosecute you. If the girl escapes with her life no real harm has been done, although you've caused a deal of unhappiness, in one way or another. For my part, I'd like to see you escape, because I'm sure this affair will be a warning to you that will induce you to give up all trickery in the future. Money would n't bribe me, as you know, but sympathy and good fellowship will. If you'll promise to skip right now, and turn over a new leaf, you are free."

"Where could I go?"

"There's a town a mile ahead of us; I can see the buildings now and then. You've money, for you offered it to me. I have n't any assistants here, I'm all alone on the job. That talk about four men was only a bluff. Push me over in the snow and make tracks. I'll tell Weldon you've escaped, and advise him not to bother you. It's very easy."

Mershone stopped short, seized the detective's hand and wrung it gratefully.

"You're a good fellow, Fogerty. I—I thank you. But I can't do it. In the first place, I can't rest in peace until Louise is found, or I know her fate. Secondly, I'm game to give an account for all my deeds, now that I've played the farce out, and lost. I—I really have n't the ambition, Fogerty, to make a new start in life, and try to reform. What's the use?"

Fogerty did not reply. Perhaps he realized the case was entirely hopeless. But he had done what he could to save the misguided fellow and give him a chance, and he was sorry he had not succeeded.

Meantime Arthur Weldon, almost dazed by the calamity that had overtaken his sweetheart, found an able assistant in his chauffeur, who, when the case was explained to him, developed an eager and intelligent interest in the chase. Fortunately they moved with the storm and the snow presently moderated in volume although the wind was still blowing a fierce gale. This gave them a better opportunity than the others to observe the road they followed.

Jones had good eyes, and although the trail of the heavy wagon was lost at times he soon picked it up again and they were enabled to make fairly good speed.

"I believe," said Arthur, presently, "that the marks are getting clearer."

"I know they are, sir," agreed Jones.

"Then we've come in the right direction, for it is proof that the wagon was headed this way."

"Quite right, sir."

This back section was thinly settled and the occasional farm-houses they passed were set well back from the road. It was evident from the closed gates and drifted snowbanks that no teams had either left these places or arrived during a recent period. Arthur was encouraged, moreover, by the wagon ruts growing still more clear as they proceeded, and his excitement was great when Jones abruptly halted and pointed to a place where the wheels had made a turn and entered a farm yard.

"Here's the place, sir," announced the chauffeur.

"Can you get in?"

"It's pretty deep, sir, but I'll try."

The snow was crisp and light, owing to the excessive cold, and the machine plowed through it bravely, drawing up at last to the door of an humble cottage.

As Arthur leaped out of the car a man appeared upon the steps, closing the door softly behind him.

"Looking for the young lady, sir?" he asked.

"Is she here?" cried Arthur.

The man placed his finger on his lips, although the wind prevented any sound of voices being heard within.

"Gently, sir, don't make a noise—but come in."

They entered what seemed to be a kitchen. The farmer, a man of advanced years, led him to a front room, and again cautioning him to be silent, motioned him to enter.

A sheet-iron stove made the place fairly comfortable. By a window sat a meek-faced woman, bent over some sewing. On a couch opposite lay

Louise, covered by a heavy shawl. She was fast asleep, her hair disheveled and straying over her crimson cheeks, flushed from exposure to the weather. Her slumber seemed the result of physical exhaustion, for her lips were parted and she breathed deeply.

Arthur, after gazing at her for a moment with a beating heart, for the mysterious actions of the old farmer had made him fear the worst, softly approached the couch and knelt beside the girl he loved, thanking God in his inmost heart for her escape. Then he leaned over and pressed a kiss upon her cheek.

Louise slowly opened her eyes, smiled divinely, and threw her arms impulsively around his neck.

"I knew you would come for me, dear," she whispered.

CHAPTER XXIV

A MATTER OF COURSE

All explanations were barred until the girl had been tenderly taken to her own home and under the loving care of her mother and cousins had recovered to an extent from the terrible experiences she had undergone.

Then by degrees she told them her story, and how, hearing the voice of her persecutor Mershone in the hall below she had become frantic with fear and resolved to trust herself to the mercies of the storm rather than submit to an interview with him. Before this she had decided that she could climb down the trellis, and that part of her flight she accomplished easily. Then she ran toward the rear of the premises to avoid being seen and managed to find the lane, and later the cross-roads. It was very cold, but her excitement and the fear of pursuit kept her warm until sud-

denly her strength failed her and she sank down
in the snow without power to move. At this juncture the farmer and his wife drove by, having been
on a trip to the town. The man sprang out and
lifted her in, and the woman tenderly wrapped
her in the robes and blankets and pillowed
her head upon her motherly bosom. By the time
they reached the farm-house she was quite warm
again, but so exhausted that with a brief explanation that she was lost, but somebody would be sure
to find her before long, she fell upon the couch
and almost immediately lost consciousness.

So Arthur found her, and one look into his eyes
assured her that all her troubles were over.

They did not prosecute Charlie Mershone, after
all. Fogerty pleaded for him earnestly, and Uncle
John pointed out that to arrest the young man
would mean to give the whole affair to the newspapers, which until now had not gleaned the
slightest inkling of what had happened. Publicity was to be avoided if possible, as it would set
loose a thousand malicious tongues and benefit
nobody. The only thing to be gained by prosecut-

ing Mershone was revenge, and all were willing to forego that doubtful satisfaction.

However, Uncle John had an interview with the young man in the office of the prosecuting attorney, at which Mershone was given permission to leave town quietly and pursue his fortunes in other fields. If ever he returned, or in any way molested any of the Merricks or his cousin Diana, he was assured that he would be immediately arrested and prosecuted to the full extent of the law.

Mershone accepted the conditions and became an exile, passing at once out of the lives of those he had so deeply wronged.

The joyful reunion of the lovers led to an early date being set for the wedding. They met all protests by pleading their fears of another heartrending separation, and no one ventured to oppose their desire.

Mrs. Merrick quickly recovered her accustomed spirits during the excitement of those anxious weeks preceding the wedding. Cards were issued to "the very best people in town;" the *trousseau* involved anxiety by day and restless dreams by night—all eminently enjoyable; there were enter-

tainments to be attended and congratulations to
be received from every side.

Society, suspecting nothing of the tragedy so
lately enacted in these young lives, was especially
gracious to the betrothed. Louise was the recip-
ient of innumerable merry "showers" from her
girl associates, and her cousins, Patsy and Beth,
followed in line with "glass showers" and "china
showers" until the prospective bride was stocked
with enough wares to establish a "house-furnish-
ing emporium," as Uncle John proudly declared.

Mr. Merrick, by this time quite reconciled and
palpably pleased at the approaching marriage of
his eldest niece, was not to be outdone in "social
stunts" that might add to her happiness. He gave
theatre parties and banquets without number, and
gave them with the marked success that invariably
attended his efforts.

The evening before the wedding Uncle John
and the Major claimed Arthur for their own, and
after an hour's conference between the three that
left the young fellow more happy and grateful
than ever before, he was entertained at his last

"bachelor dinner," where he made a remarkable speech and was lustily cheered.

Of course Beth and Patsy were the bridesmaids, and their cousin Kenneth Forbes came all the way from Elmhurst to be Arthur's best man. No one ever knew what it cost Uncle John for the wonderful decorations at the church and home, for the music, the banquet and all the other details which he himself eagerly arranged on a magnificent scale and claimed was a part of his "wedding present."

When it was all over, and the young people had driven away to begin the journey of life together, the little man put a loving arm around Beth and Patsy and said, between smiles and tears:

"Well, my dears, I've lost one niece, and that's a fact; but I've still two left. How long will they remain with me, I wonder?"

"Dear me, Uncle John," said practical Patsy; "your necktie's untied and dangling like a shoe-string! I hope it wasn't that way at the wedding."

"It was, though," declared the Major, chuckling. "If all three of ye get married, my dears, poor Uncle John will come to look like a scarecrow—and all that in the face of swell society!"

"Are n't we about through with swell society now?" asked Mr. Merrick, anxiously. "Are n't we about done with it? It caused all our troubles, you know."

"Society," announced Beth, complacently, "is an excellent thing in the abstract. It has its black sheep, of course; but I think no more than any other established class of humanity."

"Dear me!" cried Uncle John; "you once denounced society."

"That," said she, "was before I knew anything at all about it."